# THE DEADLY POLITICS OF GIVING

# THE DEADLY POLITICS OF GIVING

Exchange and Violence at Ajacan, Roanoke, and Jamestown

SETH MALLIOS

THE UNIVERSITY OF ALABAMA PRESS
*Tuscaloosa*

Typeface: Minion

∞

The paper on which this book is printed meets the minimum requirements of American National Standard for Information Sciences-Permanence of Paper for Printed Library Materials, ANSI Z39.48-1984.

Library of Congress Cataloging-in-Publication Data

Mallios, Seth, 1971–
   The deadly politics of giving : exchange and violence at Ajacan, Roanoke, and Jamestown / Seth Mallios.
        p. cm.
   Includes bibliographical references and index.
   ISBN-13: 978-0-8173-1516-0 (cloth : alk. paper)
   ISBN-10: 0-8173-1516-0 (alk. paper)
   ISBN-13: 978-0-8173-5336-0 (pbk. : alk. paper)
   ISBN-10: 0-8173-5336-4 (alk. paper)
   1. Algonquian Indians—First contact with Europeans—South Atlantic States. 2. Indians of North America—History—Colonial period, ca. 1600–1775. 3. Algonquian Indians—Wars—South Atlantic States. 4. Ceremonial exchange—South Atlantic States. 5. Spain—Colonies—America. 6. Great Britain—Colonies—America. 7. South Atlantic States—History. I. Title.
   E99.A35M35 2006
   975'.01—dc22

                                                                      2005034160

For my parents, and for my Gretchen

# Contents

# Illustrations

## Figures

## Tables

# Acknowledgments

One of my favorite apocryphal stories involves Thomas Edison and his many unsuccessful attempts at inventing the light bulb. Edison, after finally producing a bulb that gave off consistent light, was allegedly asked to reflect on his countless failures. He responded, "I had not failed; I'd just found thousands of ways that didn't quite work." In the spirit of Edison, I prefer to think of the numerous earlier drafts of this manuscript as necessary steps in the refinement of a final product that outshines yet owes much to its many prototypes. In acknowledgment of the often tumultuous publication process that can force a scholar to endure terminally ambiguous reviews, idea theft, and conference posturing, it is worth remembering that the crushing disappointment of the '46, '78, '86, and '03 Red Sox made 2004 all the more delightful.

My debt of gratitude to the many individuals who have helped me with *The Deadly Politics of Giving* is large. Fred Damon, Jim Deetz, and Jeff Hantman inspired my appreciation for historical anthropology and cultural symbolism that is at the core of this book. Bill Kelso and the *Jamestown Rediscovery* project offered me access to a wealth of resources and opportunities. The 1607 James Fort site, which produced spectacular finds on a daily basis, continues to be a remarkable and immediate testing ground for anthropological theories regarding culture contact and exchange. Although the decision to leave Jamestown and return to California was difficult, my colleagues at San Diego State University eased the transition through their unending support and enthusiasm for my work on both coasts. Joe Ball's mentorship has been a guiding light for my professional career, and Kathy Peck has routinely found clarity for me in the most convoluted of situations. The move west also reacquainted me with the ideas of some of my most inspirational undergraduate teachers from my days at Berkeley. Extended conversations with Kent Lightfoot about his recent book, *Indians, Missionaries, and Merchants,* were especially insightful during my last round of manuscript revision.

In addition to the fantastic editorial staff at The University of Alabama Press, there are three other individuals to whom I wish to express my sincere gratitude: Shane Broas Emmett, Peter Lancelot Mallios, and Gretchen Louise Mallios. First, I thank Shane for his unwavering friendship and unflappable belief in the merits of this book. Second, even if he were not my brother, Peter would still have my trust, respect, and loyalty, for he has earned them essentially and existentially. And third, I wish to thank Gretchen not only for editing the entire book and coming up with its title but also for inspiring me to begin again.

# THE DEADLY POLITICS OF GIVING

# 1

# *Introduction*

Over half a century before the Pilgrims landed at Plymouth Rock and more than two decades before Captain John Smith laid eyes on Jamestown Island, a young Virginia Indian single-handedly altered the course of European colonization in North America. "Don Luis" was the name Catholic missionaries gave to this native Algonquian; his indigenous name would forever elude the annals of history. One of the most enigmatic characters in the Age of Exploration, this Chesapeake Indian left the Middle Atlantic as a teenager to join a team of Spanish explorers. Under the tutelage of missionaries, he converted to Catholicism and ventured with the clerics across the Atlantic. While in Europe, the neophyte Don Luis met and received numerous gifts from the King of Spain. He quickly won the trust of his European hosts. In return, he vowed to lead the missionaries back into his native territory in the Chesapeake for proselytization of his kin.

Don Luis's legacy, however, was not defined by the unification of indigenous and colonial causes. Much to the contrary, his enduring moment in history was a devastating assault on the team of unarmed clerics that he led to the Chesapeake. Don Luis spearheaded the surprise attack against his fellow missionaries, personally inflicting many of the lethal wounds. Not only did the former neophyte's siege end the Chesapeake mission, it also helped to stagger Spanish colonialism in the North American Southeast and opened the door for English expansion. Had this ill-fated mission succeeded at Ajacan, located at the northern extreme of Spain's self-proclaimed La Florida territory, subsequent English ventures at nearby Roanoke and Jamestown Island would have likely been quashed by Spanish forces (Figure 1.1). In fact, if Don Luis had successfully helped to establish amicable relations between the Chesapeake Algonquians and Spanish Jesuits at his boyhood home—as was his professed original intention—

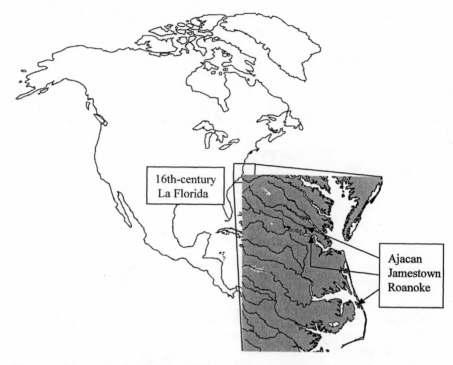

Figure 1.1. 16th-century La Florida with a close-up of the Middle Atlantic region that contains Ajacan, Roanoke, and Jamestown

it is unlikely that England's Jamestown venture would have served as a springboard for the eventual Anglo-colonization of America.

In attempting to discern the motivations for Don Luis's abrupt betrayal of the Spanish, the historical details leading up to the attack are enlightening. Don Luis had accompanied various Spanish clerics on a series of ventures in North America and Europe during the 1560s. When he returned to his childhood Algonquian home at Ajacan in the fall of 1570, relations between these Jesuits and the Chesapeake Indians initially flourished. However, some weeks into the frontier settlement, Don Luis and the other natives abandoned the missionaries and moved to the interior. Father Segura, the leader of the religious delegation, received no explanation for this desertion and went months without seeing or hearing from Don Luis. The members of the fledgling Jesuit settlement struggled to survive, trading tools for food with other neighboring natives and scavenging the local countryside for any means of subsistence.

In early February 1571, Don Luis returned. Unarmed and joined by only a few of his fellow Algonquians, he explained that they had come back to Aja-can to build a church for Segura and his followers. The neophyte stated that they wished to start construction immediately, needing only the missionaries' hatchets to begin the work. Eager to accept the Algonquians' apparent gener-osity, the clerics quickly gathered their iron tools and handed them over to the natives. Without hesitation, Don Luis seized Segura and decapitated him. Just as the senior cleric's head fell from his shoulders and struck the missionaries' makeshift altar, the other Algonquians slaughtered the remaining priests. Only Alonso de Olmos, a Spanish boy who had accompanied the Jesuits to Ajacan, was spared during the attack.

Don Luis's assault on the Ajacan Jesuits terminated the earliest recorded European attempt at settling the Chesapeake. It also marked the beginning of a series of attacks by Middle Atlantic Algonquians on European colonists that were both lethal to the settlers and highly symbolic for the indigenous popu-lation. The violent acts were distinctively Algonquian in that the method of delivery was intentional and meaningful. In fact, regional accounts of indige-nous violence during this time collectively form a cohesive story of native agency and Algonquian symbolism. Even when responding directly to English and Spanish provocation, Middle Atlantic Algonquians dealt justice in a man-ner that was culturally consistent and highly representative of indigenous so-cial norms.

Numerous aspects of the events described above at Ajacan exemplify this violent yet self-affirming Algonquian expression of identity and culture. To be-gin, even though Don Luis and his Algonquian comrades greatly outnumbered the Ajacan Jesuits, maintained a decided advantage in weaponry, and were far more familiar with the local terrain, they nevertheless deceived and annihilated the clerics in a most particular and deliberate manner. The natives choreo-graphed their execution of the Jesuits by offering them a false gift—the promise of constructing a church—and then used the Jesuits' own tools against them. In addition, the Algonquians exacted vengeance with a meaning by simultane-ously mimicking and punishing Jesuit social affronts. Specifically, the repeated Jesuit failures to reciprocate Algonquian generosity were mocked by the offer-ing of an additional gift. Lastly, the identity of the gift—the church—derided the singular missionization goal. In the end, Don Luis and his Algonquin kin gained retribution against the missionaries and simultaneously delivered a powerful message to their own community. Their violence was effective in both vanquishing specific European foes and proclaiming proper Algonquian protocol.

With a focus on indigenous cultural systems and agency, this book analyzes contact-period relations between North American Middle Atlantic Algonquian Indians and the Spanish Jesuits at Ajacan (1570–72) and English settlers at Roanoke Island (1584–90) and Jamestown Island (1607–12). It investigates the causes and consequences of conflict at these first three European attempts to settle the region, spotlighting native tactics and strategies in their dealings with colonists. Exchange, the movement of goods and services within and between societies, plays a prominent role in this study; it helps to explain some of the motivations for indigenous hostility during this period. The following pages demonstrate that Europeans and Algonquians followed strikingly different rules regarding exchange, which frequently altered overall intercultural relations.

Contact-period Middle Atlantic Algonquian exchange shared important parallels with well-documented gift-based societies in Polynesia and the North American Northwest. Cross-cultural analyses of reciprocal exchange systems reveal how non-Western socioeconomic practices and expectations differed significantly from burgeoning European market strategies in the 16th and 17th centuries. These differences contributed to intercultural strife that defined the earliest European attempts to colonize the region. At Ajacan, Roanoke, and Jamestown, European exchange transgressions against the Algonquians violated indigenous cultural norms and often incited hostile responses. Within Algonquian society, the resultant Indian attacks against the European settlers were culturally justified and effective. Again, according to their cultural construct, their lethal actions both demonstrated and avenged the European offenses.

Not all indigenous reactions to European exploration and colonization were violent (Oberg 1999; Quitt 1995). Accommodating behaviors often typified early intercultural encounters (White 1991; Dennis 1993). Even in the Middle Atlantic, early interaction witnessed great fluctuations in overall relations. For example, natives at Ajacan initially sustained the Chesapeake Jesuits in the fall of 1570 but then murdered them months later, as described. Carolina Algonquians and English scouts established amicable relations in 1584 at Roanoke Island only to have those bonds deteriorate, strengthen, and then disintegrate entirely. And in May of 1607, certain Chesapeake Algonquians immediately attacked the first Jamestown colonists while others simultaneously sustained them. In this same colony, there were then two and a half years of alternating periods of peace and hostility that ultimately gave way to three years of consistent conflict.

New insights into these differential Algonquian killings can be gained through an appreciation of the rules and consequences of non-Western gift exchange. It suggests culturally consistent explanations as to why the indigenous population might have chosen to eliminate some of the colonists and their settlements while allowing others to survive. Gift exchange is a socioeconomic system based on intertwined obligations to give, accept, and reciprocate. A detailed analysis of the nuances of native gift economies can transform these apparently erratic indigenous actions into cultural patterns within a dynamic historical process. The rules of gift exchange can help to decode seemingly cryptic Algonquian behavior. They offer an alternative narrative of past events, one grounded in indigenous economics, worldviews, and cosmologies.

The native gift economy significantly influenced relations between European colonists and America's indigenous population (cf. with Waselkov 1989; Gutiérrez 1991; White 1991; Quitt 1995; Brooks 2002). It helped to transform alliances between cultures and alter the internal hierarchy of the Algonquian world. The prosperity and longevity of colonial ventures at Ajacan, Roanoke, and Jamestown relied in part on the settlers' abilities to understand and participate in the indigenous gift economy. Individuals like Jamestown's John Smith, who had a keen grasp of native exchange tendencies, managed to negotiate extended periods of intercultural peace. On the contrary, European leaders lacking such acumen into the socioeconomics of non-Western peoples watched their settlements come to abrupt, violent, and fruitless ends.

The analyses presented here rely primarily on the details recorded by European writers during the 16th and 17th centuries. This book acknowledges the ethnocentrism of the historical authors and also addresses its own inherent biases and agendas (Jennings 1975; Dening 1980; Axtell 1981; Obeyesekere 1992; Geertz 1995; Lipsitz 1995, 1998; Sahlins 1995; Borofsky 1997; Roberts 1997). The act of chronicling the past is often oppressive to indigenous populations that faced colonization. In this analysis, it is compounded by the undeniable aura of whiteness that envelops my efforts to appreciate Algonquian motivations and perspectives from 400 years ago. Whiteness is a social category that stems from European or Western descent. The power imbued to whiteness creates a system of advantage that mandates the subordination of nonwhites (Lipsitz 1998). This system is inherently discriminatory, privileging whites over others. The meaning of a white identity can be seen in its consequences, including the social, economic, and political advantages it confers (Lipsitz 1995:369).

The Western bias that influences this analysis stems from my ethnicity, professional training, and sources of information. I am a white male, trained mostly by white males, in a discipline created by white males. White male anthropologists created the theoretical models used here, which were derived from ethnographic fieldwork conducted mostly by white males. White male settlers wrote every contemporaneous historical text detailing 16th- and 17th-century events at Ajacan, Roanoke, and Jamestown, and white males authored most of the subsequent histories regarding these settlements. I recognize the historical, cultural, and hegemonic distance between the past indigenous peoples under study here and myself. My experiential and cultural bias is inescapable; even lamenting it is an ironic consequence of being trained along Western principles (Jennings 1975:14). On the one hand the conundrum is clear: everyone is culturally biased, even those who attempt to avoid or work through it (Sahlins 1995:8). Even debates of historical accuracy—like, what *really* happened, and why did it occur in that way?—are grounded in Western notions of singular truth and objectivity. On the other hand, social pangs of guilt can lead to a cultural perspective of reverse discrimination, a sympathetic Western bias that romanticizes the dispossessed (Axtell 1981:15; Dening 1980:286). A pendulum of social consciousness often sways against established imperialistic histories in an attempt to compensate for previous disempowering narratives.

With regard to this study, guilt does not fuel my investigations of the past. I do not seek to undo European colonization, justify indigenous violence, or idealize eroded native lifeways. Rather, I endeavor to construct a narrative of culture contact that is both empirically based and culturally consistent with each group involved. Historical records, although inevitably biased, can provide significant insight into European and indigenous conceptions of exchange and violence. I treat the 16th- and 17th-century documents in this study similarly to other forms of material culture (Mallios 2004a). Applying an archaeological framework, each Euro-Algonquian exchange is examined like an item in an artifact assemblage (See Mallios and Fesler 1999; Mallios 2000, 2001; Mallios and Straube 2000). Dozens of contextual and integral attributes for each inventoried transaction are measured and recorded in an effort to isolate meaningful patterns involving exchange trends and cycles of intercultural hostility. This work contextualizes these patterns by situating them within distinct Algonquian, Spanish, and English cultural worldviews, cosmologies, and histories. Historical anthropology attempts to unite understandings of historical process with an appreciation for cultural structures and systems (Gleach 1997:7). Analytical rigor is essential in this endeavor (See Fausz 1997). Without grounding one's analysis in a robust and explicit dataset, there is a danger of highlighting exceptions to the historical and cultural patterns instead of rules (See Mallios 1998, 2001).

At the same time, I attempt to employ an appreciation of bias and agenda when scrutinizing outsider perspectives of past writers of histories (Mallios 2005b, 2007). Western Europeans penned the only contemporaneous accounts of Ajacan, Roanoke, and Jamestown. The exhaustive dataset of contact-period

Middle Atlantic intercultural exchanges examined here includes a comprehensive evaluation of all of the contemporary historical sources as to their reliability. The audience for which the particular historical text was written is also considered because writers and their audiences are inseparable in analyses of bias and perspective.

With regard to the Ajacan saga, the boy Alonso de Olmos never wrote an account of the Jesuits' 16th-century Chesapeake mission. Instead, details of the venture came from nine contemporary sources. Three of these accounts were letters sent to and from the Chesapeake during the 1570s. Fathers Segura and Quiros, the leaders of the Ajacan venture, wrote the first correspondence on September 12, 1570. Their letter, destined for the Royal Treasurer of Cuba, apprised Spanish administrators of the status of their mission, requested additional supplies, and left instructions for anyone attempting future contact with them. Spanish sovereign King Philip II responded to the clerics in a correspondence on February 19, 1571. In addition, Jesuit Father Rogel wrote a two-part letter from the Chesapeake on August 28, 1572. The initial section described the North American events he had witnessed firsthand. The second half of the letter summarized Olmos's fragmented oral accounts of Ajacan before and during the carnage. The other six contemporary accounts of Ajacan were secondhand narratives that attempted to recount Father Segura's Chesapeake experiences. Father Rogel wrote one such narrative in the 1590s. Jesuit Fathers Ribadeneyra and Carrera followed with similar accounts a few years later. A secular colonist named Martinez reflected on the Ajacan venture in 1610. Two additional Jesuit narratives were written between 1617 and 1622, one by Father Ore and the other by Father Sacchini. Since each of these secondhand summaries was based on Olmos's testimony, they presented largely congruous accounts of Segura's demise.

Roanoke settlers Arthur Barlowe, Ralph Lane, Thomas Harriot, and John White each wrote firsthand accounts of their Carolina experiences during the 1580s. Barlowe detailed the Europeans' 1584 precolony investigation of the Carolinas, and his account was corroborated by Englishmen John White and Raphael Holinshed and Spaniards Diego Hernandez de Quinones and Hernando de Altamirano. Three firsthand accounts described the first English colony at Roanoke Island of 1585–86. The Tiger *Journal of the 1585 Voyage* documented the journey of Richard Grenville and his crew to the Americas and the initial days of the English settlement. Ralph Lane, the governor of the First Colony, also kept a journal of Carolina events during his tenure. In addition, colonist Thomas Harriot wrote a report that offered descriptions of the indigenous people and goods of the Carolinas. Scattered details of Roanoke's 1586 Second Colony came from Pedro Diaz, a captured Spanish pilot, who learned of Roanoke events on the basis of what the English ship's crew told him while docked in the Carolina Sounds. John White, the leader of the 1587 Third Colony, kept journals that described the initial plight of England's final 16th-century Carolina colony. His accounts described the early days of resettlement, his decision to return to England, his inability to return to the Carolinas for three years, and his ultimate failure in locating the Lost Colony.

Many English settlers living at Jamestown Island in the early 17th century wrote detailed reports of the events they witnessed. John Smith, George Percy, Gabriel Archer, Edward Maria Wingfield, Henry Spelman, William Strachey, Ralph Hamor, and others left firsthand accounts of their Chesapeake experiences. Five of John Smith's narratives described initial English interaction with the Powhatans. Although Smith has been legitimately criticized for embellishing his narratives with fictional details of his own valor, contemporary sources frequently confirmed the general essence of his accounts (Smith et al. 1986, 1:lxiii–lxiv). Smith reported on events he personally witnessed at Jamestown from 1607 to 1609 and commented on the fate of the settlement once he had returned to England. His later texts benefited from additions by other writers (Smith et al. 1986, 1:lxv).

Smith and his writings are of particular value to this analysis of non-Western exchange practices at Jamestown for two reasons: his worldly experience leading up to the North American settlement and his role at the colony itself. First, Smith, who had been held hostage in Turkey prior to his American ventures in 1602–03, witnessed non-Western cultural norms that emphasized different exchange priorities and strategies. Flemish diplomat Ogier Ghislain de Busbecq and English poet-adventurer George Sandys each wrote detailed treatises on 16th- and 17th-century Turkish customs and noted socioeconomic practices that were distinctly non-Western in nature (Busbecq 1694; Sandys 1613). Smith's time in Turkey likely contributed to his familiarity and ease with Chesapeake Algonquian gift exchange, insight that seeped into his written accounts. Second, Smith was named Cape Merchant of the Jamestown Colony early in his Chesapeake tenure, a position whose official duties included recording all of the settlement's transactions (Smith et al. 1986, 3:83). Stripping these narratives of all but the details of individual exchanges takes Smith's reports back to what they once were—an inventory of interaction and an account of the movement of goods. Thus, Smith's texts are uniquely reflective about exchanges and as such are especially indicative of economic trends at early colonial Jamestown.

Other early firsthand Jamestown accounts include those by council presidents George Percy and Edward Maria Wingfield and an anonymous relation that was likely authored by settler Gabriel Archer. Later post-1609 accounts were penned by Colony Secretary William Strachey, council member Ralph Hamor, and colonist Henry Spelman. In sum, there is no shortage of eyewitness accounts of early Anglo-Powhatan relations in the Chesapeake. Furthermore, these colonial authors often explicitly expressed their views on intercultural relations. Whereas scholars who study the events at Ajacan often search for a voice to describe what happened and why, individuals researching the early Jamestown colony endeavor to make sense of the cacophony that results from so many simultaneous and conflicting narratives.

## Middle Atlantic Algonquians at Contact

An overview of Algonquian political culture and social structure and an examination of prized intercultural exchange goods in the Middle Atlantic are essential in properly situating this analysis of strife at Ajacan, Roanoke, and Jamestown. Nuances regarding indigenous social differentiation, power consolidation, and the flow of prestigious goods within the region played a significant role in the Algonquian conflicts with European missionaries and colonists. Recent historical, archaeological, and anthropological research continues to build upon the scholarship of past generations to present a more complete portrait of past Middle Atlantic Algonquian lifeways.

## The Chesapeake: Tsenacommacah

A large indigenous group of Algonquian speakers named the Powhatan had over 13,000 members in 31 districts centered on the James and York River basins of the Virginia Tidewater during the late 16th and early 17th centuries (Figure 1.2) (Fitzhugh 1985:188; Turner 1976, 1978, 1982). These natives called their home territory Tsenacommacah; it encompassed much of the Chesapeake. Scholars have traditionally suggested that these natives formed a complex chiefdom, following anthropologist Elman Service's models and measures of societal complexity (Service 1962; Binford 1964; Turner 1976, 1985, 1986, 1993; Feest 1978, 1987; Rountree and Turner 1998). The Powhatan had a unified and individual political chief, elite priests, ascribed status, differential mortuary practices, and a centralized tribute system. They did not form the next level of societal complexity—a state—because they lacked a rigid class system (Service 1962; Earle 1978, 1991, 1997; Wright 1984; Redmond 1998; Rountree and Turner 1998).

Powhatan society consisted of three tiers (Smith et al. 1986, 2:146–148, 150,

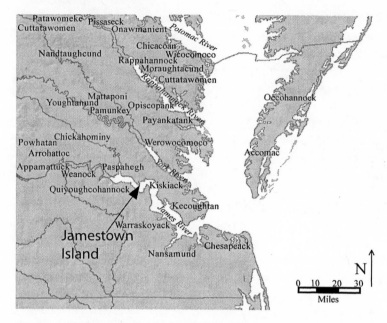

Figure 1.2. Chesapeake tribes in the Powhatan paramount chiefdom

173; Strachey 1953:63–69, 77). An elite Algonquian by the name of Wahunsona-cock was the paramount chief or *Mamanatowick* of the Powhatans during the late 16th and early 17th centuries. Upon becoming the ruler of these Chesa-peake Algonquians, Wahunsonacock took the name Powhatan. The titles "Chief Powhatan" and "Mamanatowick" are used interchangeably throughout this text. Chesapeake Algonquians attributed the word "Powhatan" to a variety of things, including the official name of the Mamanatowick, the entire native community in the region, Wahunsonacock's birth village, and the river that was next to his birth village (Rountree and Turner 1998:289). Chief Powhatan's dis-tinctive title and position have led many current scholars to label the Powhatan political structure a paramount chiefdom or paramountcy (Rountree and Turner 1998; Gallivan 2003).

The Mamanatowick's singular command over all other Algonquian tribes, despite the presence of their own local leaders, and his seemingly unquestioned rule, are the traits that define this as a paramountcy. Jamestown's John Smith emphasized that Chief Powhatan's governance of Tsenacommacah was abso-lute, writing that, "What he [Chief Powhatan] commandeth they [the other Powhatans] dare not disobey in the least thing. It is strange to see with what great feare and adoration all these people do obey this Powhatan. For at his feet they present whatsoever hee commandeth, and at the least frowne of his browe, their greatest spirits will tremble with feare" (Smith et al. 1986, 1:174).

*Weroances,* or local leaders, made up the second tier of Powhatan society. They governed individual towns and were hereditary rulers in their own right with their own source of legitimacy and authority. Weroances obtained many Algonquian luxuries as a result of their power. Chief Powhatan kept a close eye on the internal dynamics of his paramount chiefdom, frequently reassigning or replacing weroances and their followers (Strachey 1953:68). Weroances were also military commanders.

Algonquian priests defy easy classification in the Powhatan social hierarchy. Masters of native religion and medicine, their rank varied among the Chesapeake Algonquians, although most were part of this second status level. Whereas preeminent "Conjurers" who served the Mamanatowick maintained elite status, other Algonquian holy men endured a lesser rank in the Powhatan hierarchy (Smith et al. 1986, 1:171). Since the indigenous population believed that native priests could see the future, Chief Powhatan especially valued their advice in matters of conflict. Algonquian religious men commonly counseled the Mamanatowick on when to declare war and often negotiated the peace as well (Strachey 1953:104). The Mamanatowick and his weroances each claimed a purported link to the supernatural, one that was maintained and reified by the socially dead yet spiritually powerful priests (Williamson 1979, 2003).

The third and lowest Powhatan social stratum consisted of commoners. Although certain natives attained status through extraordinary performance in activities like battle and hunting, placement in the indigenous social hierarchy was mostly ascribed. Distinct Powhatan burial practices reflected the three levels of their society. The top two tiers—the political elite—were subject to elaborate funerary practices that included disemboweling, de-fleshing, and placement in temples. No such luxuries existed for commoners, who fellow Algonquians simply deposited in the ground.

A set of principles organized the Powhatan social hierarchy. Political power in Powhatan society centered on authority, warfare, and trade, each of which reflected the Chesapeake Algonquin cultural worldview (Gleach 1997:28). These principles were essential in the development of the Powhatan paramount chiefdom as well (Rountree and Turner 1998:284–285; Carneiro 1978:207–208). There was also a dual sovereignty to Powhatan society: one spiritual and the domain of the conjurers and the other mundane and controlled by the weroances (Williamson 2003). Only the Mamanatowick united the two realms, a rare union that gave him the ability to exercise his power in nearly all matters.

The Powhatan tribute system both reflected and maintained Algonquian authority. By 1607, the individual tribes within the Powhatan chiefdom were not socially equal and competed for higher status through offerings made to the Mamanatowick (Rountree 1989:100). Smith's writings include details about native offerings that indicate that lesser Algonquian weroances paid "tribute of skinnes, beads, copper, pearle, deare, turkies, wild beasts, and corne" to Chief Powhatan (Smith et al. 1986, 1:69). In fact, Jamestown colonist William Strachey asserted that the Mamanatowick could command up to 80 percent of the goods produced by his people as tribute (Strachey 1953:81). Chief Powhatan did not accept the overwhelming majority of his followers' goods; he was, however, offered them (Williamson 2003:154).

Scholars have traditionally noted that the Powhatans did not maintain a redistributive chiefdom because elite natives kept and circulated most of the tribute goods among themselves (Schwerin 1973:10; Earle 1978:15, 181; Kirch 1984:134; Rountree 1989:14, 1990; Rountree and Turner 1998:269). An appreciation for Powhatan cosmology may contradict this notion, or at least lead to the redefinition of what redistribution was. Generalized exchange entails the continual passing on of goods, which bonds an entire community of individuals (Sahlins 1972; Damon 1980, 1990, 1993). Chesapeake Algonquians believed that elite Powhatan were buried with prestigious goods with the intent of giving them to Powhatan deities in the afterlife. If Powhatan deities passed these goods back to the third tier of Powhatan hoi polloi through the creation or reincarnation of these items in the material world, then the Powhatan tribute system would be redistributive. Almost all of the people who received redistributed goods from the Mamanatowick—priests, lower chiefs, warriors, and the planters of his cornfields—worked for him and gave him items as well. The Mamanatowick's reciprocity was more personal than all encompassing; individual services for him rarely went unrewarded while membership in his society did not guarantee gifts from him.

The Powhatans offered items to the Mamanatowick as gifts to acknowledge their subjugation to him. On the basis of these offerings, he responded with a promise of alliance and protection. Chief Powhatan also offered return gifts—elevated status, favors, and redistributed goods (Rountree 1989:111). The Mamanatowick divided the tribute he received. He placed some of the goods in warehouses, offered various items to his followers, and sacrificed isolated offerings to Algonquian deities. According to their customs and beliefs, the gifts to the supernatural were reciprocation for the gifts of creation and good fortune and further united all Powhatan peoples.

## Powhatan Political Development

Powhatan scholars disagree as to the timing and causes of the formation of the paramount chiefdom. Some assert that complexity arose from local and long-term evolutionary processes unrelated to European contact. Lewis Binford compared the Powhatan to other indigenous populations within the region in terms of environmental and social factors—resource zones, population, settlement complexity, and so forth—and concluded that the complex chiefdom arose as an independent adaptation to these stresses (Binford 1964). E. Randolph Turner agreed and maintained that the rise of the Powhatan complex chiefdom resulted from significant population growth during the Late Woodland period (A.D. 900–1600) and the pressure it put on prime growing and harvesting areas (Turner 1976, 1985:209–211, 1993:92–93). Stephen Potter saw material parallels between the independent development of Algonquian culture in the Potomac Valley from A.D. 1350 to 1500 and the rise of the Powhatan complex chiefdom from A.D. 1500 to 1600. He concluded that since European Contact did not cause the formation of the small chiefdoms along the Potomac River, the development of Powhatan social complexity also unfolded independent of European influence (Potter 1982, 1993; Rountree and Turner 1998:286).

On the contrary, others claimed that the restructuring and unification of native groups into a more complex and cohesive unit resulted from the presence and consequences of Europeans, especially the devastating toll that their diseases took on indigenous populations (Feest 1966, 1978; Fausz 1985:235; Axtell 1988:181; Hudson and Tesser 1994; Dent 1995; Kupperman 2000:36–37). Historian J. Frederick Fausz and ethnohistorian Helen Rountree did not perceive these points of view as mutually exclusive (Fausz 1977; Rountree 1990; Rountree and Turner 2002). Rountree acknowledged both explanations, writing that, "Though the chiefdoms may have been a 'natural' development, a major factor in the rise of the paramount chiefdom in eastern Virginia was the increased military threat the people of the region felt from Europeans and other Indians alike, possibly coupled with social disruption caused by epidemics" (Rountree 1990:10).

Drawing on comparative settlement pattern studies and multiple lines of evidence, Martin Gallivan's recent archaeological study on the development of the Powhatan chiefdom also accommodated both viewpoints (Flannery 1972; Lightfoot 1984; Lightfoot and Jewett 1986; Gallivan 2003). Through detailed analyses of sites along the James River Valley, he identified marked changes in Algonquian settlement dynamics—including degree of sedentism and amount

of storage use—that reflected a distinctively new and different set of social or-
ganizational processes in effect between A.D. 1200 and 1500 (Gallivan 2004:43).
In addition to those already mentioned, other recent studies also relied on archaeological evidence to substantiate the rise of social complexity in the region
(Hodges 1993; Potter 1993; Klein 1996; De Boer 1998; Klein and Sanford 2005).

Chief Powhatan achieved the powerbase of his burgeoning complex chiefdom through two primary means—inheritance and force. In the middle to late
1500s, he inherited between six and nine districts along the James and York Riv-
ers (Fitzhugh 1985:188). Toward the end of the 16th century, Chief Powhatan
subjugated over 20 additional neighboring groups and made them part of his
chiefdom (Smith et al. 1986 1:173). Strachey gave specific details of the subjugation process, which included the conquering of villages and frequent forced
relocation of their inhabitants. He explained: "Upon the death of an old Weroance of this place [the town of Kecoughtan] . . . Powhatan taking the advantage subtilly stepped in, and conquered the People[,] killing the Chief and
most of them, and the reserved he transported over the Riuer, craftily changing
their seat, and quartering them amongst his owne people . . . the remyne of
those lyving haue with much sute obteyned of him *Payankatank*, which he not
long since dispeopled" (Italics original; Strachey 1953:68). The adversarial nature of political growth in Powhatan society made for a divisive community.

## Powhatan Foreign Relations

In addition to the Mamanatowick's supreme position over smaller Powhatan
tribes and their populations, he also negotiated strained and often treacherous
relations with adjacent indigenous groups. As of the early 1600s, Powhatan adversaries included the Monacans west of the Fall Zone on the James River, the
Mannahoacks at the start of the Rappahannock River, and the Massawomecks
beyond the head of the Potomac River (Smith et al. 1986, 1:165). Powhatan relations with adjacent groups fluctuated, and the Mamanatowick occasionally
allied himself with former adversaries (Strachey 1953:105–106; Rountree 1993).
In addition, there was one distinct tribe in the heart of Powhatan territory
that refused to acknowledge the Mamanatowick's rule. Two thousand semi-
independent Chickahominies lived in the heart of Powhatan territory on the
James/York peninsula and avoided complying with the centralized Powhatan
tribute system. Unlike the usual weroance that reported to Chief Powhatan, an
internal group of independent priests and elders governed the Chickahominies
(Williamson 2003:71). While members of the other districts in the paramount
chiefdom gave frequent offerings to the Mamanatowick, the Chickahominies

often failed to participate in the tribute system. Detailing an important distinction for the overall thesis of this text, Chief Powhatan contemptuously described these politically independent natives who rarely offered gifts as having "the nature of a Merchant" (Smith et al. 1986, 1:71). The resistance of the Chickahominies serves as an important reminder to scholars as to the frequent dissension within the Powhatan paramount chiefdom. Although there was only one Mamanatowick in the early 1600s, he and most likely the position itself were relatively new, and weroances occasionally undermined his power (Gallivan 2003:26).

## The Carolinas: Ossomocomuck

Approximately 100 miles to the south of the Powhatan paramount chiefdom, six different tribes of Algonquian-speaking natives occupied the region that today is recognized as North Carolina (Figure 1.3). These late 16th-century tribes were the Roanoacs, the Secotans, the Chawanoacs, the Weapemeocs, the Moratucs, and the Croatoans. They formed a series of politically independent small-scale chiefdoms, each with its own weroance, and entirely separate from their Powhatan neighbors to the north. This region, known collectively as Ossomocomuck, had over 7,000 indigenous inhabitants by the time Europeans attempted to colonize the area (Kupperman 1984:50). Chief Wingina led the Roanoacs, governing villages at Roanoke Island and settlements located on the mainland between the Alligator River and Croatoan Sound. When Wingina was recuperating from war wounds, his brother Granganimeo ruled. The Secotans maintained villages from the Pamlico River basin to Albemarle Sound. The Chawanoacs, led by Chief Menatonon, lived on the Upper Chowan River and sustained the largest tribe in the area with over 2,500 people (Kupperman 1984:75). The Weapemeocs, led by Chief Okisko, had settlements north of Albemarle Sound between the Chowan River and Currituck Sound. Chief Pooneno ruled the Moratucs who lived along the Roanoke River between the Chawanoacs and Secotans. The Croatoans built their towns on Croatoan Island and on other islands in the Outer Banks south of Roanoke. Manteo, a native prince who visited England, led the Croatoans during the end of the 16th century.

Compared to the Powhatan, less is known about the Algonquians of the Carolina Sounds. The many observations recorded by Chesapeake colonists during the early 17th century dwarf the early historical accounts of Carolina's indigenous population for at least two reasons. First, the duration of Jamestown's permanent settlement was significantly longer than the brief and un-

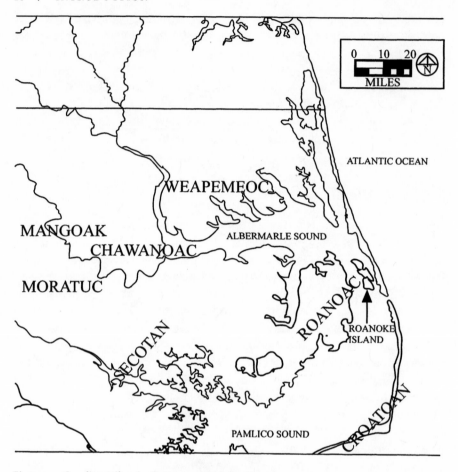

Figure 1.3. Carolina tribes in Ossomocomuck territory

successful initial colonies at Roanoke Island. Second, the fascination and curiosity with native populations that peaked during the early 1600s had long since passed by the time permanent European settlement succeeded in the Carolina Sounds (See Quitt 1995). The many volumes that Age of Exploration writers penned about America's indigenous peoples diminished when plans for colonial expansion were already well in action.

Nevertheless, active historical, anthropological, and archaeological research in the region has produced substantive information regarding the Carolina Algonquians at contact (Monahan 1995; Ward and Davis 1999; Herbert 1999; Davis and Child 2000; VanDerWarker 2001; Mallios 2004b). Overall, Carolina and Chesapeake Algonquians shared many similarities in the late 1500s and early 1600s. The most notable exception between Chesapeake and Carolina Algonquians was the presence and unified rule of the Powhatan Mamanato-wick. Both groups successfully farmed, using slash-and-burn agricultural techniques. They shared common hunting, fishing, and foraging methods as well. Carolina and Chesapeake Algonquians were mostly sedentary, although each kept seasonal villages. In addition, these groups possessed like social structures (Fausz 1985:227). They were matrilineal, shared a common polytheistic belief system as well, and men of both groups were polygynous, frequently taking more than one wife. The two chiefdoms also engaged in hierarchically based mortuary rites (Quinn 1955; Fausz 1977; Feest 1978; Merrell 1979).

Close reading of the historical documents reveals that contact-period indigenous societies were not monolithic cultural blocks. As a result, this analysis emphasizes the separate identity of individual polities within the different Algonquian societies. Recognition of tribal distinctions within the contact-period Middle Atlantic can help to clarify seemingly incongruous or contradictory actions. Although individual native tribes in both the Chesapeake and Carolinas were a part of larger indigenous political systems, their intracultural alliances were far from regular or unconditional. The arrival of various European missionaries and colonists only served to complicate their already highly intricate and volatile web of relations. At Ajacan, Roanoke, and Jamestown, colonists and missionaries often mistook the different indigenous tribes for one another; modern scholars must take extra care not to repeat this error.

## Prestigious Exchange Goods

Before European contact, Middle Atlantic Algonquians cherished a variety of luxury goods, placing a special emphasis on copper, iron, antimony ore, shell beads, and pearls (Rountree 1989:55). These goods were rare, and some of them came from distant territories. Following the arrival of the Spanish and English in the Chesapeake, European goods were often highly valued by the Powhatan, and these items played a prominent role in the indigenous tribute system. The Algonquians passed foreign goods immediately up their social hierarchy (Rountree 1989:55, 56).

The indigenous population valued European goods for a variety of reasons. Since these items were found almost nowhere else in the Middle Atlantic, the natives prized them for being exotic. In addition, Chesapeake and Carolina native groups commonly equated the distant origins of certain goods—whether from Europe or remote North American sources—with the supernatural. They cherished trade items that originated from areas beyond the region (Miller and Hamell 1986:319–320). Furthermore, some of the European goods physically resembled native spiritual items, and the indigenous population often included these particular items in their ceremonies (Miller and Hamell 1986:315).

Contact-period Algonquians obtained three kinds of European goods— metals, tools, and small items. Smith summarized that, "for a copper kettle . . . a few toyes . . . and hatchets . . . [the Powhatans] will sell you a whole Countrey" (Smith et al. 1986, 3:276). Like Columbus, Vespucci, and dozens of other European explorers of the Americas, Smith often characterized the Western goods that the natives desired as trash (Smith et al. 1986, 3:29, 160; Jehlen and Warner 1997:13–14, 20). Although English colonists at Roanoke and Jamestown frequently equated the items they traded to the Algonquians with garbage, they knew that it was precisely the exchange of these materials that sustained them. With provisions regularly spoiled aboard transatlantic ships and a dearth of farmers among the settlers, successful trade with the natives was essential for the colonists.

The English learned quickly at Roanoke Island in 1584 of the supreme value the Algonquians placed on various metals. When displaying the goods they intended to trade, explorer Arthur Barlowe and his men witnessed how the Roanoacs revered tin. Barlowe reported that, "When we shewed him [Roanoac Chief Granganimeo] all our packet of merchandize, of all things that he saw, a bright tinne dishe most pleased him, which he presently tooke up, & clapt it before his breast, & after made a hole in the brimme thereof, & hung it about his necke, making signes, that it would defende him against his enemies arrows" (Quinn 1955:101). Since there are no direct historical analogs or archaeological examples of metal armor among contact-period natives in the North American Southeast, Granganimeo's words to Barlowe were most likely figurative. The metal pendants likely "defended against his enemies' arrows" by symbolically protecting against death. They were symbols of alliance, prestige, and strength, each of which contributed to a veneer of impenetrability.

Carolina and Chesapeake Algonquians publicly demonstrated their status by the copper they wore. Pierced copper pieces hung around the neck or on the arms distinguished elite natives from commoners. Powhatan warriors frequently received copper from the Mamanatowick in return for military service. Successful combatants accumulated much of the prestigious goods. Smith observed the prominence of copper among elite individuals in the Powhatan world and noted that natives would often wear together around the neck a prized possession—"a broad peece of copper"—and a fruit of their aggression—"the hand of their enemy dried" (Smith et al. 1986, 1:161). In addition, the Powhatans frequently offered copper to their deities by ceremoniously throwing it in the river.

Copper also figured prominently in Powhatan beliefs regarding the afterlife. They maintained that copper ensured the soul's safe haven once the body expired. Chesapeake natives buried their leaders with many high-status goods, including this metal. The Powhatans even took the cadavers of their chiefs and stuffed their bodies with copper beads. The presence of copper in Powhatan burials served as a distinction between chiefs and non-chiefs. The non-elite Powhatans believed that they possessed no afterlife. Smith noted that, "the common people they suppose shall not live after death, but rot in their graves like dead dogs" (Smith et al. 1986, 1:172). Thus, copper segregated people whose spirits would live forever from those individuals whose souls would expire following their corporeal death. Overall, copper gorgets were the ultimate Algonquian insurance policy; they protected elite natives by rewarding warriors, appeasing gods, and enabling spiritual immortality.

European colonists came to Jamestown in the early 1600s with substantial stores of trimmed copper ready for exchange. They had learned from their comrades' Carolina experiences 20 years earlier. Roanoke's Thomas Harriot emphasized the indigenous population's high regard for copper and specified that the Jamestown colonists should bring it to the Americas in specific pre-trimmed forms for trading. Harriot detailed that colonists should bring in their trading kit, "10 seven-inch squares, 5 seven-inch circles, 20 six-inch squares, 10 six-inch circles, 40 four-inch squares, 20 four-inch circles, and 100 three-inch squares" (Quinn 1977:432–434). The three colonies that the English attempted to plant at Roanoke Island in the 1580s failed in establishing a permanent settlement, but lessons learned from those ventures gave the colonists at Jamestown a better chance at survival.

Copper influenced trade and relations in other indigenous groups as well, not just among Algonquian tribes. For instance, anthropologist Jeffrey Hantman included the Monacans, a Sioux-speaking group to the west of the Powhatan chiefdom, in his discussion of the Chesapeake's copper trade. Although historical records chronicled little of Powhatan/Monacan relations during the 16th and 17th centuries, they indicated that when the English arrived at Jamestown Island the Powhatans and Monacans were adversaries (Smith et al. 1986, 1:165). Hantman posited that the Powhatan/Monacan copper trade played an important role in early English/Powhatan relations. With no indigenous copper in his own territory, Chief Powhatan likely relied on exchange with natives in the Great Lakes region, western North Carolina, and nearby Monacan territory, all of whom tapped copper sources (Hantman 1990:685, 1993). The arrival of the English in 1607 and their many copper goods gave the Mamanatowick an opportunity to rid himself of his dependence on hostile Monacan neighbors (Hantman 1990:685). Abundant copper from the colonists freed Chief Powhatan of indebtedness to the Monacans along his western border and increased his strength outside of the chiefdom. The Mamanatowick also bolstered his power by controlling the flow of copper within his territory. He offered these prestigious goods to the weroances, thereby placing them firmly in his debt.

Copper was so highly valued that it influenced relations between indigenous neighbors in the Middle Atlantic, often helping to quell or incite feuds. Parallels existed between the Chesapeake copper trade of the early 1600s and copper exchange in the Carolinas during the late 1500s. In both cases, copper entered the region from the west, either from alleged sources in the Blue Ridge Mountains or the Great Lakes. Additionally, non-Algonquian groups—the Monacans for the Powhatans and the Mangoaks for the Ossomocomuck tribes—played a role in controlling the influx of the prestigious items (Quinn 1955:281). Just as the Powhatans often simultaneously fought with and depended on the Monacans, the Roanoacs maintained similarly ambiguous relations with neighboring tribes. Historical records suggested that Chesapeake and Carolina Algonquians permitted English intrusions into their homelands because doing so allowed access to an abundant supply of copper from apparently friendly sources. The Europeans' plentiful copper stores gave the natives an opportunity to exchange with individuals other than antagonistic neighbors.

While natives embraced new relations with European colonists in an attempt to unburden themselves of resource dependency on antagonistic indigenous neighbors, English settlers also sought alternative resources when they ventured to the Americas. One of England's goals in settling the Middle Atlantic was to relieve itself of a similar material dependence on nearby European rivals. English colonial advisor Richard Hakluyt, the younger, wrote in 1578 of his country's desire to avoid economic restraints. He asserted that, "[England] should not depend on Spain for oil, sacks, resins, oranges, lemons, Spanish skins, &c. Nor upon France for woad [wood], basalt, and Gascoyne wines, nor on Eastland for flax, pitch, tar, masts, &c . . . we should, by our own industries and the benefits of the soil there, cheaply purchase oils, wines, salt, fruits, pitch, tar, flax, hemp, masts, boards, fish, gold, silver, copper, tallow, hides, and many commodities" (Jehlen and Warner 1997:58). Overall, just as the English came to the Americas in the hopes of freeing themselves from economic dependence on political adversaries, they unknowingly offered the Powhatans, and perhaps the Roanoacs as well, a chance for the same sort of relief.

Iron tools were another European trade good that Algonquians prized.

These items were produced by a technology that the Algonquians did not possess. Whereas English copper maintained a similar form to other copper obtained by the Algonquians and could be freely substituted for it, European tools made from iron represented just the opposite. Natives sought them precisely because they were so different from indigenous materials.

The third category of goods that Algonquians acquired from the Europeans consisted of a wide variety of small objects. Middle Atlantic settlers frequently referred to their knickknack trade items as "bables," "toys," "trash," "trifles," and "trinkets" (Smith et al. 1986; Quinn 1955). These goods included beads, bells, trinkets, needles, pins, and dolls. Archaeological excavations at many contact-period sites have verified the importance of glass beads and other small finds as staples in the European trade kit (Bradley 1977; Deagan 1987; Fairbanks 1968; Fitzgerald et al. 1995; Francis 1988; Harris 1982; Huey 1983; Karklins 1974, 1985; Kenyon and Fitzgerald 1986; Lapham 1995, 2001; Miller et al. 1983; Mitchem and Leader 1988; Pearson 1977; Ross 1974; Smith 1976, 1983; Smith and Good 1982; Wray 1983). Smith often singled out beads in his descriptions of trinkets offered to the Algonquians. In fact, he went out of his way to embellish the significance of certain beads, informing the Mamanatowick that the blue ones he offered were "composed of a most rare substance of the colour of the skyes, and not to be worne but by the greatest kings in the world" (Smith et al. 1986, 2:156).

In exchange for European copper, tools, and trinkets, Algonquians gave food to the settlers. Indigenous foodstuffs included a variety of wild game as well as corn and bread. Although the Powhatans offered animal skins to the English as well, nourishment remained the native population's one and only true export good of value for the colonists (Smith et al. 1986, 1:67, 165). Each of the European crews at Ajacan, Roanoke, and Jamestown did not intend to farm or hunt in the Chesapeake. They planned in advance on subsisting off of exchange with the indigenous population for food. And while the Algonquians initially agreed to part with their foodstuffs, the production and consumption of food in indigenous societies had additional symbolic significance that when unrequited had severe consequences.

## Other Factors for Strife

Modern scholars generally agree that there was a clash of cultures at Ajacan, Roanoke, and Jamestown, and that this clash resulted in violence (Fausz 1977, 1981, 1984, 1985, 1987, 1988, 1990; Kupperman 1980, 1984, 1995, 2000; Axtell 1981, 1985, 1988, 1992, 2001; Fitzhugh 1985; Gradie 1988, 1990, 1993; Rountree 1989,

1990, 1993; Williamson 1992, 2003; Quitt 1995; Gleach 1997). This work endeavors to build on these explanations and pinpoint the particular ways in which they clashed—the dynamic sequence of conflicts and resolutions—and suggest explanations for how and why natives, colonists, and missionaries mediated the clash. Inhabitants of the contact-period Middle Atlantic both participated in and transformed these cultural events and social structures. Members of each culture actively reiterated and altered their societies (Bourdieu 1977a; Giddens 1979; Sahlins 1981, 1985; Mintz 1985; Gleach 1997; Clifford 1988; Wolf 1997; Gallivan 2003).

Other scholars' interpretations of the events at Ajacan, Roanoke, and Jamestown have served as important intellectual context for the ideas presented in this book. Current explanations of Don Luis's decision to eliminate the Jesuits consistently emphasize singular motives for both the Algonquian abandonment and the attack. Historian Charlotte Gradie maintains that Jesuits impinged on Algonquian cultural norms and suffered the fatal consequences of social encroachment (Gradie 1988:149). Rountree suggests that Don Luis struggled with loyalties to both Jesuits and Algonquians, feared the public humiliation that would inevitably come from being labeled a traitor by either group, and, as a result, chose to eliminate the weaker Jesuit contingency (Rountree 1990:17). On the contrary, anthropologist Frederic Gleach claims that Don Luis brought together Powhatan and Jesuit worlds by giving the Jesuits that which they desired the most: martyrdom (Gleach 1997:95). The analysis presented here suggests that two distinct socioeconomic affronts by the Jesuits resulted in two different and chronologically separate indigenous punishments: abandonment and death. In addition, the particular way in which the natives killed the missionaries showcased important symbolism that reflected the Jesuit mistakes.

Eminent Roanoke historian David Beers Quinn asserted that the 1580s rift between the colonists and Carolina Algonquians resulted from European pressures on the native corn supply and the severe effects of Western diseases on the indigenous population (Quinn 1949, 1955, 1970, 1971, 1973, 1974, 1977, 1978, 1979a, 1979b, 1979c, 1983, 1984, 1985, 1990, 1994; Quinn and Ryan 1983). He also suggested that the settlers' conquering mentality worsened the situation (Quinn 1985:237). Other historians such as Edmund Morgan, Fausz, and Karen Kupperman, and archaeologist Ivor Noël Hume have built on these ideas and showed how the particular policies and actions of certain colonists fomented English/ Algonquian antagonism (Morgan 1976; Kupperman 1984; Fausz 1985; Noël Hume 1994). This analysis, too, incorporates the work of Quinn; it frames his catalysts for strife in terms of inter- and intracultural exchange and exchange-based relationships.

Many scholars have suggested causes for English/Powhatan hostility during Jamestown's inaugural years. The body of research on this topic is substantial, offering multiple theories to explain the tensions following this next round of culture contact in the Middle Atlantic. Namely, factors related to settlement location, natural calamities and their effects on local resources, exchange behaviors, the particular identity of individual exchange agents, and inundation of exchange goods have all been put forth as catalysts for the ensuing deterioration of Anglo-Powhatan relations.

Rountree maintained that English expansion in the summer of 1609 induced widespread native attacks (Rountree 1993:170, 183; 1990:55; Potter and Waselkov 1994). Historian April Hatfield offered specific details in support of this theory, noting that the colonists during this time had acquired an Algonquian town that was especially symbolic to the Powhatan. She asserted that losing the particular town that was Chief Powhatan's birthplace and the former capital of Tsenacommacah was a direct challenge to the Mamanatowick's authority that provoked immediate Algonquian hostilities (Hatfield 2003:250).

Archaeologist Dennis Blanton pinpointed severe drought conditions during 1606–12 that likely strained intercultural relations (Blanton 2000, 2004). His work noted that each of the first three European attempts at settling the Middle Atlantic—Ajacan from 1570 to 1572, Roanoke Island from 1584 to 1590, and Jamestown from 1607 to 1612—occurred during times of significant drought. Far from an environmental determinist, Blanton emphasized that these environmental strains exacerbated existing tensions between Europeans and Algonquians.

Fausz, anthropologist Margaret Holmes Williamson, historian Martin Quitt, and Gleach all pointed to inadequate English reciprocation as a reason for Algonquian aggression (Fausz 1985, 1988, 1990:18, 20; Williamson 1992:303; Quitt 1995:231; Gleach 1997:129). Quitt identified five stages of deteriorating exchange-based relations that preceded violence during the 1607–09 time period: unbalanced hospitality and gift giving, unbalanced gift giving and barter, balanced barter, trade embargo, and forced trade (Quitt 1995:244). This analysis endeavors to build on Quitt's ideas in two ways. First, it links the intercultural exchange deteriorations directly to violence. Second, it refines his model of historical exchange transformations as cyclical and somewhat self-generative instead of linear (Oberg 1999:6). Fausz also noted how John Smith repeatedly eased intercultural tensions (Fausz 1990:24). Likewise, Gleach saw Smith's return to England as a significant loss for the colony because it removed their most important intercultural liaison with the Powhatan (Gleach 1997:128).

Fausz, Potter, and Hantman stressed the role of copper in American rela-

tions. They believed that economic practices of the English and their consequences inspired the natives to strike (Fausz 1985:239; Potter 1989:157; Hantman
1990:685–686). Potter asserted that by 1609, English traders had inundated the
Powhatan with copper, diminishing its value and the power of local Algonquian leaders (Potter 1989:157). Both Potter and Hantman identified a change
in Powhatan relations with the settlers following copper's debasement (Potter
1989:157; Hantman 1990:686).

Each of these explanations for intercultural conflict at Jamestown listed
above has a direct tie to the central themes of this book. They all involve the
intricacies of exchange. This text endeavors to use the aforementioned ideas of
other scholars in conjunction with a rigorous examination of the primary historical texts to add to ongoing debates about why Anglo-Powhatan relations
broke down in 1609. Understandings of conflict at Jamestown Island shed light
on other intercultural struggles in the contact-period Middle Atlantic as well.

# 2
# Gifts and Commodities

## The Gift Economy

Whereas a gift is a simple and direct something-for-nothing offering, gift exchange is part of an elaborate social and economic system with rules and consequences. Gift exchange dictates that there is no such thing as a free gift. There are always strings attached. Of the many scholars who have studied exchange, none figure more prominently here than anthropologist Marcel Mauss. On the basis of extensive description from existing ethnographies, Mauss developed a theory in the 1920s regarding gift-exchange systems. He built his model on cross-cultural social and economic elements from contemporaneous societies in Polynesia, Melanesia, and the American Northwest, as well as past Roman, Hindu, Germanic, Celtic, and Chinese civilizations. Although he did not explicitly detail a commodity-exchange system in his text, Mauss frequently contrasted gift economies he analyzed with the market economy in which he lived. For example, when describing similar gift-exchange systems from different geographic regions and time periods, Mauss lamented the early 20th-century European commodity-based system, led by "the cold reasoning of the merchant, the banker . . . the capitalist," and other members of "*Homo oeconomicus*" (Mauss 1990:75, 76).

Mauss posited that gift- and commodity-exchange systems do not mutually exclude each other. Gift giving exists in a commodity economy and sale occurs in a gift-based system (Mauss 1990:76; Otnes and Beltramini 1996:3; Carrier 1990). He maintained, however, that ultimately one of these two types of exchange dominates every economy (Malinowski 1922). In fact, Mauss declared that the predominant exchange system—either gift-based or commodity-based—works its way into every aspect of a given society (Mauss 1990:29). The particular type of economy is thus inseparable from the group's total social phenomenon (Hyde 1983:xv). Mauss grounded his work in the concept of the social fact, referring to a phenomenon so pervasive that it could not be reduced to the sum of the individuals in a specific culture and was independent from their consciousness. He developed these ideas from the writings of his mentor and uncle, anthropologist and sociologist Émile Durkheim (See Durkheim 1938).

## The Form and Motivations of Gift Exchange

The riddle of the gift lies in the uncertainty of what drives it—generosity or obligation. Mauss believed that both forces were catalysts for gift giving. The transactions may take the form of unconditional and unsolicited offerings, but these gifts are, quite to the contrary, mandatory. Paradoxically, there is nothing free about the seemingly free gift and nothing altruistic about the giver. The duality of the gift system is that its participants make offerings both because they want to and because they are obliged (Mauss 1990:71).

Mauss poetically captured this balance between desire and obligation, writing that, "Society always pays itself in the counterfeit coin of its dream" (Bourdieu 1997c:231). His metaphor captures two distinct aspects of the gift. "Society paying itself" is a reference to obligatory reciprocity, the mandatory offerings made by individuals in the gift economy. One must participate and give presents. The fact that giving is required makes the act seem more like a payment than a gift. Yet the exchange is made "in the counterfeit coin of its dream." The offering maintains the superficial form of pure something-for-nothing generosity, dubiously appearing to be a selfless act of altruism. Although these transactions are indeed mandatory, they are indistinguishable from magnanimity. The dream is generosity; the hidden reality is an obligation to give (Mallios 2005a).

## Gift-Exchange Obligations

When passing gifts back and forth, participants in the gift economy must satisfy three obligations: they have to give, receive, and reciprocate. Failure to fulfill any of these duties results in a loss of social status (Mauss 1990:39–41). In gift societies, there is no greater personal devastation; loss of prestige is tantamount to spiritual death. Yet gift-based gains to individual prestige are twofold. First, a gift offering signifies the belief that the giver is and will remain fortunate enough and held in favor by the supernatural to do without the item. The public offering of the gift draws attention to this good fortune, thereby raising the individual's status. Second, the giver's prestige also increases once the gift is accepted because the offering obliges the recipient to return the favor. Indebtedness holds paramount importance because members of a gift economy endeavor to maximize the number of debts owed to them (Gregory 1982:19). The identity and utility of the goods is secondary to the relational hierarchy that they help construct. Gifts, therefore, serve as powerful tools that create and manipulate relationships between people.

The gift economy does not permit an offering to be rejected. Acceptance, however, is burdensome. One avoids the status-reducing paradox by giving first. In this self-starting exchange system, one can take control of the situation, gain status, and mandate reciprocity by giving first. The rules of the gift economy also dictate a timeline for reciprocity. Once a gift is received, the recipient must make a return offering within a given amount of time. In between gift acceptance and reciprocation, indebted individuals are in the unenviable position of being obliged. They must show deference and reverence for their benefactor, or else they could be accused of being ungrateful (Bourdieu 1997b: 199). Improper reciprocation violates the gift economy, resulting in immediate status reduction and social castration for the individual that transgressed the gift-exchange system (Mauss 1990:42).

Positioning in the social hierarchy controls the movement of gifts. High-rank individuals exchange high-rank gifts because they can repay them and because these gifts and gift partners reaffirm their dominant social position (Mauss 1990:57). Likewise, low-rank individuals do not have the economic viability to give or receive high-rank gifts and must exchange low-rank gifts (Bourdieu 1997b:192). Thus, gift exchange facilitates, maintains, and mediates social hierarchies (Godelier 1996:44, 2002:22; Strathern 1988:107).

### The Spirit of the Gift

Gifts are active; each offering retains some of the giver's soul even after the item is exchanged (Mauss 1990:11–13, 49). Mauss noted that many non-Western cultures hold the belief that gifts literally contain the donor's spirit. These presents are alive. In fact, Mauss took the Maori (Polynesian) concept of the "hau"—the spirit of the gift—and extended it cross-culturally to be the key mechanism of all gift economies (Sahlins 1972:153). Mauss's incorporation of the hau as a motivation for all enabled him to answer the question—why do people reciprocate?—that stumped anthropologist Bronislaw Malinowski (Weiner 1992:45). Gift recipients are obligated to reciprocate because they have accepted the vital essence of the giver along with the present. When the actual gifts embody the exchange partners, it creates spiritual bonds between people that must be maintained by reciprocation and future interaction (Parry 1986:457).

Since gifts are living things that carry the giver's spirit, each gift exchange is not a transfer of private ownership. The exchanges resemble a loan more than a sale (Mauss 1990:44). Gifts are inalienable. Furthermore, these gifts must continue to be given. In this way, inalienable gifts perpetuate gift exchange and the further inalienation of these items. No one can own the spirited gift. It must be continuously passed on to others. The temporary possessors of the gift infuse it with their soul as well. Each giver's spirit remains in the gift even after it is given (Damon 1980, 1990, 1993). The perpetual movement of individual offerings reveals that the gift is simultaneously from everyone and from no one in particular (Shapiro 1997:275).

In societies where gift giving dominates, individuals refuse to restrict the movement of any particular type of good. They give, accept, and reciprocate nearly everything (Mauss 1990:14; Godelier 2002). The offerings link all givers and recipients in every aspect of society (Mauss 1997:29). This seemingly infinite transference of gifts and debts creates groups of people who are permanently allied and perpetually interdependent (Gregory 1982:19).

### Gift-Exchange Violations

Violating the gift-exchange system is more than a simple economic transgression. Mauss explained that, "To refuse to give, just as to refuse to accept is tantamount to declaring war; it is to reject the bond of alliance and commonality" (Mauss 1990:13). Anthropologist Claude Lévi-Strauss articulated the profound and inherent link between exchange and hostility, stating that, "Exchanges are peacefully resolved wars, and wars are the result of unsuccessful transactions" (Lévi-Strauss 1969:67). Failure to fulfill the first two economic obligations—giving and accepting—may result in aggression from the rejected exchange partner and status degradation. To ignore the third gift-economy duty—reciprocation—often leads to a different ramification. Failing to make a sufficient return offering enslaves delinquent givers to their benefactors (Mauss 1990:42).

Straining or severing gift-based alliances also undermines the gift economy. When a gift-exchange partner is removed or alienated, the transactions dependent on those same relations cease. Any action that disrupts the alliance, including theft, violence, or privileging the social rivals of one's exchange partner, dissolves the accord. A relationship strained by transgressions of the gift economy requires immediate attention. Without it, the exchange-partner bonds are in danger of being negated, potentially leading to strife.

## The Commodity Economy

Principles of private ownership guide a commodity-exchange system (Althusser and Balibar 1968; Appadurai 1986). Whereas individuals in a gift economy attempt to acquire debt and obligation from each other, participants in a commodity-exchange system desire an immediate acquisition of material wealth (Bloch and Parry 1989:3; Irigaray 1997:175). Karl Marx defined the commodity concept, labeling it "the elementary form of capitalist wealth" (Marx and Engels 1977:91). The exchange of inert, inactive, soulless, alienable goods provides the basis for commodity economies (Ollman 1971:133). Commodities have no spirit; in fact, their collective alienation reflects the amputation of the soul of the previous owner from the item (Nemoianu 1985:323).

People in a market-based commodity-exchange system individually own the goods involved in a sale. With each subsequent transaction, they transfer ownership completely. Whereas a gift carries its history through each inalienable transfer, alienable commodity transactions break the links between exchanges. The only relationship of significance is the economic one between equated exchange values (Kopytoff 1986:68). The individuals engaged in the trade are de-emphasized (Gregory 1982:42). Any person can buy or sell any item at any time. The transactors are reciprocally independent; their relationship is only a momentary alliance that will terminate upon the conclusion of the trade (Marx and Engels 1977:91). Furthermore, the closeness of the relationship between commodity-exchanging individuals and their respective status does not necessarily change with each purchase. Like buying a soda from a vending machine, the objects that are transferred in each exchange do not significantly impact the identity and prestige of the transactors or their relationship. There is no economically based interpersonal bond; in essence, it is entirely antisocial (Bellamy 2003:96).

### Commodity-Exchange Violations

Violations of commodity-exchange systems disrupt the equitable flow of goods. Theft moves merchandise in only one direction, and it denies the requisite equation of exchange values. Whereas stealing violates the gift economy by undermining relationships between allied exchange partners, it transgresses commodity economies by failing to provide compensation for the merchandise.

Transactions that flood an exchange market and drive prices down disrupt the commodity economy as well. Subtle changes in the availability of goods are not necessarily economic infractions because they are an integral part of the supply-and-demand system. Drastic or repeated inundation of specific goods, however, strips the items of their exchange values and obstructs access to wealth. Overloading a market with goods diminishes their export value and exchange worth. In extreme cases, an over-supply severely disadvantages one group of individuals and jeopardizes their economic viability in the market-exchange system. The consequences of these actions can include a decrease in the demand of the over-supplied good, immediate price lowering, and reduced overall interaction.

## Contrasting Gift and Commodity Models

Anthropologist Chris Gregory summarized the differences between gift- and commodity-exchange models in terms of the goods involved and the relationships between the participants. He wrote that, "Commodities are *alienable* objects transacted by aliens; gifts are *inalienable* objects transacted by non-aliens" (Italics original; Gregory 1982:43). One is a sale by strangers; the other is a loan between familiars. Some scholars dispute this dichotomy (e.g., see Healey 1986; Cheal 1988; Stirrat 1989; Gell 1992; Strathern 1992). Others have extended it into a binary opposition for all human mental structures (Thomas 1991). Gregory treated gift and commodity exchange as opposites, contrasting the giving of inalienable goods between permanently allied and perpetually interdependent transactors with the trading of alienable goods between momentarily allied and perpetually independent transactors (Gregory 1982:43). The present discussion incorporates exchange form into Gregory's dichotomy (See Stirrat 1989:94). Commodities are alienable objects *traded something for something* by aliens; gifts are inalienable objects *given something for nothing* by nonaliens. The gift mandates a return gift and is essentially an exchange of something for something; yet it takes the meaningful form of something for nothing.

These economic models are ideals. In actuality, gift- and commodity-exchange systems are not mutually exclusive (Bloch and Parry 1989:10). Societies contain a blend of both types with one particular system dominant. As a result of the realities of mixed economies, commodity strategies impact gift-based economies, and gift nuances alter market-centered exchange systems. In a theoretically perfect gift economy, no insufficient return offering could exist because attention would be focused entirely on the relationship between exchange partners. Therefore, any item, regardless of utility, would suffice. In practical economic transactions, however, the gift recipient must perceive and acknowledge the offering as sufficiently valuable. Similarly, gift-system transgressions frequently influence market exchange. For example, a strained interpersonal bond—classified earlier as the result of a gift-system transgression—

can alter the exchange tendencies of individuals in a commodity economy. The interpersonal relationships impact a commercial decision. For example, shoppers may avoid a particular market if they dislike the salespeople there. Ultimately, any economic violation that influences the value of the transacted goods or the link between exchange partners can leave its mark on any exchange reality in between the abstract gift and commodity extremes.

The pleasure of giving—be it the heartwarming sensation of generosity, the security of ensuring reciprocity, or the delight in gaining status—is often counterbalanced by a sincere displeasure in receiving. Essayist, philosopher, and poet Ralph Waldo Emerson warned his readers that, "the hand that feeds us is in some danger of being bitten" (Emerson 1997:26). Likewise, Mauss noticed a similarity between the roots of the words "gift" and "poison" in the languages of many societies (Mauss 1997:30). The linguistic parallel intimates that accepting a gift can be analogous to ingesting poison. Like Emerson, Mauss acknowledged both positive and negative aspects of gift exchange, noting the alliances it could build and the shame it could cast (Strathern 1988; Bloch and Parry 1989:9; Parry 1989:65). Regardless of the intentions of the giver, each transfer of something for nothing significantly impacts exchange partners. Gift giving alters every relationship.

## Methodological Application of Economic Theories

Using criteria established from the theoretical exchange models, this study quantified and classified every historically documented intercultural exchange that occurred at contact-period Ajacan, Roanoke, and Jamestown (See Mallios 1998). An exchange was defined as the movement of any good or service from one individual or group to another. The transactions were classified as gifts or commodities on the basis of three factors: (1) exchange-partner relationship, (2) exchange-item alienation, and (3) exchange form (Table 2.1). *Exchange-partner relationship* referred to whether the exchange occurred between individuals who were repeatedly allied, frequently interdependent, and of similar intracultural rank, or between people who were momentarily allied, temporarily interdependent, and of different intracultural rank. *Exchange-item alienation* determined whether the goods were continually passed on to others following the exchange, or kept and individually owned by the initial recipient. *Exchange form* distinguished an exchange that appeared as a something-for-nothing gift from a transaction that resembled a something-for-something trade.

The historical records provided definitive information regarding these three

Table 2.1. Exchange classification criteria

| | Exchange-Partner Relationship | | Exchange-Item Alienation | Exchange Form |
|---|---|---|---|---|
| Gift-Exchange System | Exchange partners are repeatedly allied | Exchange partners are frequently interdependent | Exchange partners are of similar rank | Exchange items are inalienable; the goods are continually passed on to others | The exchange is a something-for-nothing gift |
| Commodity-Exchange System | Exchange partners are momentarily allied | Exchange partners are frequently independent | Exchange partners can be of different rank | Exchange items are alienable; the goods are kept and individually owned | The exchange is a something-for-something trade |

socioeconomic measures for most of the transactions. Whereas other criteria could not be determined on an individual basis for most exchanges, these three measures appeared consistently and formed the basis of the quantitative analyses. Qualitative analyses were performed on those details that were not consistently discernable. The findings and their ramifications on the link between exchange and violence are discussed in the conclusion.

This study described every transaction in terms of 31 attributes, divided into eight groups (A–H). Each attribute was posed as a question. The first group of queries (A) provided the basic details of the exchange, including the who, what, where, and when of each transaction. The second attribute group (B) asked whether the transaction occurred between aliens, those who are strangers, or nonaliens, those who are familiars. It investigated issues of rank and alliance. In a gift economy, exchange partners are necessarily of similar rank. They frequently interact with one another, and this interdependence forges an alliance between the two. Social status and affiliation are of no consequence to those individuals who participate in a commodity economy. Thus, gift exchange is theoretically exclusive to nonaliens, and commodity exchange can occur between any two individuals, familiar or not.

Group C discerned whether the goods exchanged were alienable or inalienable. This determination hinged on what happened to the items after they were transacted. Ownership of alienable commodities is restricted to each individual sale and does not necessarily get passed on to others. On the contrary, the inalienable gift always continues to be given and is transferred to others. The fourth group of inquiries (D) elicited information regarding the form of the exchanged goods. Gifts appear superficially as voluntary offerings; commodities are transacted simultaneously one for the other. Group E concerned the internal timing of the exchange. Group F was self-scrutinizing, examining the separateness of each exchange. Historical records occasionally combined several transactions together. The questions in this attribute set warned if the possibility existed that multiple exchanges were being treated as individual transactions. Answers to these queries also noted if there was a chance of this analysis over-separating exchanges. This group of questions also pinpointed the exact exchange terms used in the historical records.

The seventh group of inquiries (G) critiqued the sources that provided the historical information. It asked questions regarding the completeness, reliability, and originality of each source. The completeness of the exchange description was based on what percentage of the previous 23 questions was answered definitively by the historical records. The reliability of the exchange accounts was based on the directness of the information and the amount of supporting evidence. This set of questions also was directed at determining whether the historical account was plagiarized. The study presented here attempted to avoid inflating the legitimacy of verified testimonies if they are merely copied accounts.

This analysis used multiple factors to classify exchanges as gifts or commodities. It created and employed a fluid typology that allowed for comparisons. For example, it could address which was more of a gift, an alienable offering between strangers or an inalienable trade between allies. By doing so, this analysis placed transactions on a continuum of reciprocal exchange between theoretical ideals of "the gift" and "the commodity." Perfect gift exchange consisted of an inalienable something-for-nothing offering between nonaliens of the same rank; perfect commodity exchange was an alienable trade of something-for-something between aliens. Although all of the exchange attributes were essential to the classificatory process, six in particular—questions 11 to 16 from groups B, C, and D—determined the specific placement of each transaction on the exchange continuum. The eighth set of attributes (H) quantified and performed calculations on information from questions 11 to 16 that determined the exchange's exact spot on the transaction spectrum.

The specific questions asked within each attribute group are as follows:

Group A: Who, what, where, and when
  (A1) What was the number of this exchange chronologically?
  (A2) Who wrote about this exchange and when was it written?
  (A3) Who were the natives involved in the exchange?
  (A4) Who were the Europeans involved in the exchange?
  (A5) What was exchanged from the native(s) to the European(s)?
  (A6) What was exchanged from the European(s) to the native(s)?
  (A7) When were the goods exchanged?
  (A8) Where were the goods exchanged?
Group B: Exchange-partner relationship
  (B9) What were the intracultural ranks of the natives involved in the exchange?
  (B10) What were the intracultural ranks of the Europeans involved in the exchange?
  (B11) Hierarchically, were these intracultural ranks similar?
  (B12) Had these same individuals ever exchanged any goods or services before this transaction?
  (B13) Did these same individuals ever exchange any goods or services following this transaction?

Group C: Item alienation

(C14) Were the goods that went from the natives to the Europeans ever reclaimed by a previous owner or given to a third party?

(C15) Were the goods that went from the Europeans to the natives ever reclaimed by a previous owner or given to a third party?

Group D: Exchange form

(D16) Did the exchange take the form of something-for-nothing?

Group E: Exchange timing

(E17) Which goods were exchanged first, those from the natives or those from the Europeans?

(E18) Was the exchange completed immediately?

(E19) Who initiated the exchange, the natives or the Europeans?

Group F: Exchange separateness

(F20) Was the exchange immediately preceded by another exchange between the same individuals?

(F21) Was the exchange immediately followed by another exchange between the same individuals?

(F22) Could this be a reference to more than one exchange?

(F23) What exact words were used in the historical records to describe the exchange?

Group G: Exchange source critique

(G24) How complete was the exchange account?

(G25) How reliable was the exchange account?

(G26) Did the exchange details come from a plagiarized account?

Group H: Exchange calculations

(H27) What was the sum, after appropriate weighting, of the responses of questions 11 to 16, with 0 for "no" and "ø," 1/2 for "?," and 1 for "yes"?

(H28) What percentage of questions 11 to 16 answered definitively with a "yes" or a "no" answer had an affirmative (gift-oriented) response?

(H29) Did this exchange fall into the category of "other" because it was not completed, because it was based on duplicitous motives, or because neither group in the transaction attempted to transfer debt or wealth?

(H30) Was this a violent exchange that resulted in death, abduction, or abuse?

(H31) Based on the calculations in questions 27 and 28 and the disqualifying conditions in questions 29 and 30, was the exchange more gift-like or commodity-like, did it fall into the categories of "other" or "other/violence," or did it elude all of these labels and receive the designation "commodity/gifts"?

Through the quantification and classification of every intercultural exchange, this analysis revealed general trends regarding historical exchange at Ajacan, Roanoke, and Jamestown. The patterns were not subtle. An overwhelming number of intercultural exchanges initiated by the Algonquians were gifts. In fact, Algonquian gifts with the Jamestown colonists outnumbered trades by nearly 10 to 1. This evidence indicated that the Chesapeake's indigenous population was far more accustomed to giving gifts than trading. Conversely, intercultural exchange initiated by the English was dominated by trade. The missionaries' economic practices alternated between gift and commodity exchange. These patterns are discussed and explained at length in the conclusion of this text, which immediately follows the three case-study chapters.

# 3
# Ajacan

An understandably defeatist attitude permeates many scholarly discussions of Ajacan. This stems from a variety of factors, but it is primarily due to the paucity of historical records that exist regarding this attempted settlement and the questionable details within them. To begin with, the Jesuits resided at Ajacan for less than six months, which included a period of isolation for nearly half of that time. Thus, the amount of interaction with local Algonquians and the window of opportunity to record this interaction were limited. Apart from the brief duration of the failed mission, scholars also encounter a challenge regarding the historical accuracy of the Ajacan narratives. The lone European eyewitness testimony regarding Father Segura's demise at the hands of ex-neophyte Don Luis is questionable. It came from Alonso de Olmos, the traumatized youth who had forgotten most of his Spanish by the time natives returned him to his people 18 months after the Algonquian attack. Scholars also struggle with rampant revisions of Ajacan's history by those who documented it. Subsequent accounts from contemporaneous Floridian authorities dwelled more on establishing the martyrdom of Father Segura and his brethren than piecing together the sequence of actual events (Quinn 1977:283; Mallios 2005b, 2007). Archaeological endeavors have added little insight to the story; the exact location of Ajacan remains a mystery.

The present analysis of conflicting cultural exchange systems revitalizes otherwise stifled investigations of these historical records. With it, seemingly innocuous economic details spring to life and form a meaningful pattern. They identify an additional potential factor in determining why the Chesapeake Algonquians murdered the eight Spanish Jesuits. The violence can be seen as culturally justified and symbolically meaningful punishment for successive missionary violations of the indigenous gift economy.

## The History

Spanish/Chesapeake Algonquian interaction can be grouped into the following five periods:

(1) Prelude to Ajacan,
(2) Initial amicability at Ajacan,
(3) Indigenous abandonment of the clerics,
(4) Algonquian hostility, and
(5) Spanish retribution.

### Period I: Prelude to Ajacan

During the late 15th century, Pope Alexander VI granted King Ferdinand V and Queen Isabella I of Spain economic claim to American territories and goods (Fernández-Armesto 1991:137). In the Bull of 1496, he required that the Spanish monarchs take spiritual responsibility for the indigenous inhabitants of these lands as well (Fernández-Armesto 1991:137; Codignola 1995:195; Headley 1995: 252). As a result, both material and religious considerations fueled Spain's plans for the Americas. Although the *Nina, Pinta,* and *Santa Maria* did not carry a clergy member on their joint voyage in 1492, Christopher Columbus brought priests on his second transatlantic journey (Bannon 1967:39). Following these first Spanish ecclesiastics in the Americas in November of 1493, almost every subsequent ship that sailed from Europe to the Western Hemisphere over the next century had a missionary as part of its crew (Bannon 1967:39).

Spanish exploration included parts of southern North America during the first half of the 16th century (Hoffman 1980, 1986, 1990; Milanich 1990:7; Ewen 1990:83–91; Hudson et. al 1990:107–119; Dye 1990:211–222). Inland voyages by Francisco Vazquez de Coronado and Hernando de Soto broadened Spain's colonial horizons (Quinn 1977:262). Even 50 years after Ponce de Leon's initial 1513 Spanish landing in La Florida, however, Spain was still without a settlement in the North American Southeast (Milanich 1999:78). In the middle 1560s, Admiral Pedro Menéndez de Avilés, serving as the first Governor of Spanish Florida, annihilated a small French colony in northern Florida. He further secured the territory for Spain by establishing a series of military outposts in the area (Milanich 1999:78). The Bahia de Santa Maria, later named the Chesapeake Bay, held many potential riches for European colonizers. Hopes of finding an accessible waterway to the Far East through North America, establishing easily defended ports for frequently pirated ships, and obtaining valuable native goods kept Menéndez eager to expand the Spanish empire northward past the entrance of the Chesapeake Bay (Lewis and Loomie 1953:5).

Only the secular colonist Martinez described the earliest historically recorded encounter between Spanish explorers and the Chesapeake's indigenous population. Referring to an event that occurred in 1561, he reported that, "Pedro Menéndez [de Avilés] . . . discovered on the coast a large bay [the Chesapeake]. He entered further into the harbor and sailed up into it. When the Indians saw the boats, they came alongside in canoes and boarded the flagship. There His Excellency [Menéndez] . . . regaled them with food and clothing" (Lewis and Loomie 1953:5). This expedition started the saga of Ajacan, as it marked the first recorded interaction between the Spanish and Don Luis's tribe.

Martinez's claim that Menéndez led this expedition into the area is questionable (Lewis and Loomie 1953:18). The assertion that Menéndez captained a 1561 venture contradicted a statement Menéndez himself wrote in a letter to King Philip II on January 30, 1566. In this correspondence, Menéndez declared that he wanted to see the Chesapeake "with his own eyes," suggesting that he had not been there yet (Lewis and Loomie 1953:18). None of the other contemporaneous accounts indicated that Menéndez led this crew. These discrepancies suggest that Martinez's details regarding Menéndez heading the venture cannot be relied upon for certain accuracy.

Regardless of who led the 1561 Spanish contingency, once this individual finished his initial round of offerings to the natives, negotiations began on a second transaction—European acquisition of the chief's son. The Spanish sought permission from the Algonquian leader to take the native prince from his home and have him travel the world with them. Martinez wrote that the Europeans "pledged . . . to return him with much wealth and many garments" (Lewis and Loomie 1953:156). Although some modern scholars have recently suggested that the Spanish kidnapped the Algonquian boy, Father Ore and Father Sacchini each confirmed that the indigenous youth was not abducted; rather the chief's son voluntarily joined the Spanish (Axtell 2001; Price 2003; Townsend 2004; Lewis and Loomie 1953:179, 221). The Algonquians had already eagerly accepted gifts offered by the Spanish leader. According to gift-exchange norms, they were now indebted. Thus, the Spanish leader provided a convenient avenue for the natives to repay their debt when he made his request to have an Algonquian accompany his crew.

Beyond indebtedness, the indigenous chief had numerous gift-based reasons to accept the Spanish leader's arrangement (cf. Lightfoot 2005:85; Milliken 1995:221; Hoover 1989:397; Monroy 1990:33; Font 1931:246–253). First, the Spanish leader promised more exotic gifts upon the Algonquian prince's return. Second, the acceptance of a return gift by the Spanish was likely to ensure further reciprocation and interaction. A continuous gift cycle would secure a steady influx of precious European goods into Algonquian society through the native chief. This would allow him to control the flow of these prestigious items, a power that indigenous leaders often sought and cherished. Third, the Spanish commander demonstrated his relative wealth and high status to the Chesapeake natives by offering exotic gifts. The Algonquian leader could reaffirm his own social dominance within the native world by obtaining this elite associate as an ally and exchange partner. Fourth, the act of visiting foreign places was empowering for indigenous travelers (Helms 1988:13). By gaining familiarity with the outside world, the chief's son would return home with rare knowledge that his fellow Algonquians prized. Fifth, during his ventures to foreign lands, his indigenous comrades would view him as a hero, which granted prestige to his family during the prince's absence (Helms 1988:16). Gifts, promises of additional gifts, and elevated social status softened the impact of the temporary departure of the chief's son from Algonquian society. The native prince would become an important figure in history, but would only be recorded by the name given to him by the Spanish, which was Don Luis.

There is disagreement regarding whether Don Luis's family knew of his decision to join the Europeans. Martinez maintained that the young native's father orchestrated the deal. On the contrary, Sacchini declared that, "None of [his] family knew of" the arrangement (Lewis and Loomie 1953:221). Ore mentioned that many natives came aboard, implying that once these Algonquians left the European vessel they passed on news of the young prince's decision to join the Spanish (Lewis and Loomie 1953:179). Neither Ore's story nor the other sources detailed why these natives would not inform Don Luis's relatives of his departure. Overall, the written records suggested that the Algonquian's family knew that Don Luis left with the Spanish.

After the Spanish departed the Chesapeake with Don Luis, the vessel is recorded to have gone either to Mexico or to Spain. Father Carrera and Father Rogel asserted that the new convert then visited King Philip II in Spain after he was baptized in Mexico. However, Martinez, Ore, and Sacchini insisted in their respective relations that the European explorers brought the native prince immediately to Spain from the Chesapeake. They reported that as a guest of the monarch, members of the royal court educated, baptized, and sustained him, and then the neophyte returned to the Americas. The events that followed Don Luis's baptism—either in Mexico or Spain—offered insight into which of these two scenarios is more likely. It is firmly established that soon after his religious conversion, the neophyte volunteered to lead a group of Dominican friars to Ajacan. The missionaries accepted his offer and in 1566 journeyed toward the Chesapeake. Multiple historical accounts of this trip, including one written by the pilot of the vessel, revealed that Don Luis and the clerics did not reach their intended destination, and the ship's pilot redirected the vessel to Spain. Carrera and Rogel's narratives described each leg of Don Luis's trip to and from Europe. According to their accounts, the Algonquian prince traveled from Ajacan to Mexico with the Spanish crew in 1561 and sailed from the Chesapeake when the 1566 attempt at establishing a mission at Ajacan failed. They recorded that Menéndez then brought Don Luis back to Mexico between 1566 and 1569. Don Luis, Father Segura, and the rest of the second Ajacan-mission crew then departed the Caribbean in 1570 for the Chesapeake.

Martinez, Ore, and Sacchini put forth a significantly different account of Don Luis's travels. In asserting that the native prince was taken directly to Spain from the Chesapeake, Martinez, Ore, and Sacchini alleged that Don Luis visited Europe twice—first, prior to 1566 when King Philip II entertained him; and second, following a failed attempt at reaching Ajacan in 1566. Their respective narratives, however, did not describe each leg of Don Luis's travels should he have made two separate European voyages that they have alleged. They detailed his initial pre-1566 journey from the Chesapeake to Spain and implied a return trip to Mexico with Menéndez. Other sources confirmed the neophyte's trip to Europe in 1566. What Martinez, Ore, and Sacchini did not provide was an explanation of how Don Luis ended up back in the Caribbean for the second and final trip to Ajacan in 1570. As a result of this omission, it is more likely that the native prince traveled to Mexico from the Chesapeake and was baptized there in the Americas as opposed to Spain.

Although the historical records offered contradictory accounts, the more complete narratives insisted that Don Luis was taken directly to Mexico. Once there, Dominican friars educated and baptized the Algonquian. Named after the Viceroy of Mexico, Don Luis de Velasco, the Chesapeake novice continued to work with the friars in and around the Caribbean during the early to middle 1560s.

As both Algonquian prince and neophyte, Don Luis succeeded in balancing gift exchange and missionary practices. Don Luis made an offer to Admiral Menéndez, volunteering to lead the Dominican friars to Ajacan in order to help them convert his former tribe. This offer of labor would erase his debt, solidify his bond with people who had previously aided him, and further his interaction with an individual of similar high status. In addition, Don Luis's potential gift was one of the few reciprocal services he could offer that would be perceived as useful to the missionaries, as it furthered the conversion process.

Menéndez accepted the neophyte's offer in 1566 and ordered that preparations be made for a team of soldiers and clerics, including Don Luis, to missionize the Chesapeake. Again, the two primary accounts of this unsuccessful voyage to Ajacan maintained strikingly different explanations for the venture's failure. Gonzalo Solís de Merás, a 16th-century Spanish chronicler of La Florida and the admiral's brother-in-law, wrote a report blaming the missionaries. He accused the clerics, who allegedly "could no longer endure such a difficult life," of encouraging the soldiers and the pilot "into a conspiracy" that rerouted the ship to Spain (Connor 1925, 1:207; Barcia 1951:128, 132). Yet pilot Pedro de Coronas's account faulted neither the crew nor himself. He charged the neophyte with a deficient memory, maintaining that Don Luis was unable to locate his home. Coronas insisted that he and his shipmates scoured the Chesapeake for Ajacan, and that ultimately, high winds drove the Spanish vessel out of the bay.

Based on a regulation enacted by Menéndez following this debacle, it seems he was skeptical of Coronas's explanation. Immediately after the attempt to set up a mission at Ajacan in 1566 was aborted, the admiral enacted new punishments regarding the transportation of clerics. He established rules "for the most severe penalty . . . for any captain who would make an unauthorized voyage carrying a missionary" (Lewis and Loomie 1953:24).

The unsuccessful attempt at finding Ajacan was one of a set of challenges facing the venture. La Florida's Governor Menéndez had returned to Spain in 1567 and stayed until 1568. This proved to be a particularly difficult time for the North American colonial empire he was attempting to develop. Deteriorating relations with the indigenous population dissolved completely. The French revisited the North American Southeast as well, avenging the deaths of their comrades at Fort Caroline with the destruction of the Spanish garrison at San Mateo (Quinn 1977:277–278). Before returning to La Florida, Menéndez obtained the services of the Society of Jesus in hopes of converting American natives. The purported zeal of the newly formed Jesuit Order and their success in Portuguese colonies across the globe, combined with a letter from Pope Pius V written in August of 1569 that urged the admiral to continue the soul-saving quest, led Menéndez to turn to these particular clerics for help with the missions of La Florida (Quinn 1977:279).

After failing to locate Ajacan, Coronas, his crew, and Don Luis sailed across the Atlantic and arrived in Spain in 1566. As soon as the neophyte met the King, Philip II began regaling him with an assortment of gifts, including fine clothing and food. These offerings again placed Don Luis in debt to an elite Spanish benefactor. The neophyte acknowledged the debt and attempted to repay it through a reciprocal offering. For the second time he volunteered to return with a group of missionaries to his homeland and convert his native tribe. The Algonquian chief's son repeated the practice of presenting his services to high-status individuals, making the offer to the Father Vice-Provincial and the monarch. Don Luis convinced Father Segura that together they could successfully convert the neophyte's former Algonquian community. Segura obtained royal approval for the plan, and in 1570, Don Luis guided the Jesuit missionaries into the Chesapeake.

Segura sought native conversion through the construction, maintenance, and operation of a standing Jesuit mission in the Chesapeake. By taking Don Luis to Ajacan, Segura hoped that the young man would help proselytize his native kin as Don Jaime had done with his former Floridian tribe at Tequesta years earlier (Lowery 1911:339–358; Lewis and Loomie 1953:93). The rest of the small Jesuit crew was made up of Father Luis de Quiros, Brothers Gabriel Gomez, Sancho Zaballos, and Pedro Mingot de Linares, lay catechists Cristobal Redondo, Gabriel de Solis, and Juan Baptista Mendez, and Alonso de Olmos, the teenage son of a Santa Elena colonist studying with the clerics (Lewis and Loomie 1953:27). In contrast to previous missionary undertakings in La Florida, no soldiers joined the group bound for Ajacan. Furthermore, only Segura and Quiros had participated previously in proselytization ventures.

Father Segura had intentionally surrounded himself with inexperienced colleagues and a dearth of military personnel. Father Juan de la Carrera, in charge of providing supplies for the Ajacan mission, and other Spanish officials vehemently disputed Segura's choice of crew (Lewis and Loomie 1953:133). A series of recent Jesuit deaths at native hands caused Carrera great uneasiness with sending an unarmed group into foreign territory (Lewis and Loomie 1953:133). Through Quiros, Segura explained to Carrera and his other critics why he refused to take any troops or clerics with previous American conversion experience to Ajacan. During a tour of Floridian missions in the late 1560s, Segura had witnessed overzealous soldiers and jaded missionaries repeatedly undermine native proselytization (Lewis and Loomie 1953:25). He felt that military members often antagonized the indigenous population, while a priest with even the slightest bit of seasoned skepticism jeopardized the entire clerical endeavor. Segura prevented undedicated missionaries from enticing or being enticed by military personnel to mutiny by excluding both from his crew.

Carrera also disapproved of the supplies that Segura intended to take to the Chesapeake. Segura had sent Quiros to Carrera with an extensive list of ornate religious items that he wished the designated clerical outfitter to provide for the mission. Carrera feared that an abundance of eye-catching holy goods at Ajacan would encourage the natives to steal and hence would lead to conflict. Carrera begged Segura to reconsider but ultimately supplied him with all of the items he requested, including "the best and richest articles . . . in the way of chalices, monstrances, and vestments" (Lewis and Loomie 1953:133).

In contrast to the many religious goods loaded on board the Jesuits' vessel, the missionaries brought few barrels of food on their trip to Ajacan. Segura later lamented that he and his compatriots "were ill-provisioned for the journey" (Lewis and Loomie 1953:90). When the voyage to the Chesapeake took longer than expected, Segura shared the limited missionary foodstuffs with the entire ship's crew. Their dwindling food supplies did not overly trouble Segura, however, as the clerics planned to live on the charity of the indigenous Algonquians from the outset of the venture (Lewis and Loomie 1953:89). Segura insisted that the Jesuits' Ajacan trek continue "despite such scanty stores" (Lewis and Loomie 1953:90).

## Period II: Initial Amicability

Once in the Chesapeake, but not yet at Ajacan, the missionaries received regular gifts of food from the indigenous population. Quiros remarked that, "the Indians whom we met . . . would give us from their poverty" (Lewis and Loomie 1953:92). This interaction continued the string of Spanish/Algonquian gift exchanges. Almost without exception, the intercultural transactions consisted of mutual something-for-nothing offerings between individuals of like status who repeatedly engaged one another. Quiros emphasized that the next exchange that occurred between the two groups disrupted relations. He explained that, "By a bit of blundering (I don't know who on the ship did it) someone made some sort of a poor trade in food. I see now [September 12, 1570] the misfortune which followed . . . now they [the natives] are reluctant when they see they receive no trinkets for their ears of corn. They have brought the ears of corn and other foods and asked that they be given something when they handed them over. They say they have done that with others" (Lewis and Loomie 1953:92).

As soon as an anonymous Spanish crewmember traded some of his belongings for food, the natives changed their behavior. They now voiced their transaction expectations, expressing a desire for compensation from the missionaries. The "poor trade" that Quiros described provided additional clues about the nuances of earlier transactions along the James River. Before the trade, the natives initiated the exchanges by "handing" over corn to the foreigners. After the trade they still gave first, yet the Algonquians also began to ask for reciprocation.

The "poor trade" was a commodity exchange, a something-for-something trade between independent and momentarily allied exchange partners. It infuriated Segura. Quiros did not refer to this exchange as "poor" and the product of "blundering" because it resulted in the acquisition of insufficient goods or the relinquishment of high-quality items. The poorness to which he referred described the trade process itself and the fact that a trade had occurred. Commodity exchange between the Jesuit crew and the Ajacan natives violated the missionary economy. The clerics believed that it undermined the conversion process and jeopardized the purported purity of the natives with elements of European greed. The "poor trade" did not contain an economic transgression; its very essence was an exchange-system violation.

Segura knew that the missionaries' survival depended on native charity. Quiros echoed this sentiment, asserting that, "We must live in [Ajacan] . . . with what the Indians give us" (Lewis and Loomie 1953:92). Segura and Quiros cherished their singular purpose of converting nonbelievers to Christianity and detested any actions that impeded their goal (Ignatius 1959:108; 1951; Longridge 1955; Martin 1987). In their view, trade with the Ajacan natives hindered them in two ways. On a spiritual level, the clerics were concerned that Western avarice would undermine proselytization. On a more practical level, the Jesuits had few items with which to barter. Their supplies consisted almost entirely of religious goods, used exclusively for sacred purposes (Lewis and Loomie 1953:132–133). They could not be profanely sold to pay for foodstuffs.

Immediately following the "poor trade," Segura prohibited future commodity exchanges with the natives. In the postscript to the clerics' letter, Quiros detailed Segura's mandate. He wrote, "Take care that whoever comes here in no wise barters with the Indians, if need be under threat of severe punishments, and if they should bring something to barter, orders will be given that Don Luis force them to give in return something equal to whatever was bartered, and that they may not deal with the Indians except in the way judged fitting here" (Lewis and Loomie 1953:92). Segura attempted to undo any commodity exchange by forcing individuals who traded with the Algonquians to make an additional gift to the natives of equal value to the goods relinquished. In mandating that each European pay double for any Algonquian items acquired, the Jesuit leader undermined the essence of a commodity exchange by making it inherently inequitable.

Segura made two qualifications on his order forbidding exchange with the Algonquians. First, dealings with the natives had to be "in the way judged fitting here," referring to their mission of proselytization. Therefore, the clerics only allowed gift-based transactions that increased conversion potentials. Second, the nontrade order concerned only the native group the clerics intended to proselytize. Segura forbade Jesuit trade with the Ajacan locals but allowed it with natives who fell outside of their immediate conversion interests (Lewis and Loomie 1953:109). This meant that the group that was sustaining the Ajacan missionaries did not receive any material benefits for their efforts while surrounding tribes did. Using Don Luis as their guide and interpreter, the Chesapeake missionaries focused their proselytizing attempts on his former tribe, while occasionally engaging in exchange with his neighbors who contributed to the Algonquian tribute system described earlier.

When Segura and his colleagues finally anchored and came ashore on September 10, 1570, members of the native population celebrated the return of Don Luis. Segura and Quiros wrote that the Algonquians "seemed to think that Don Luis had risen from the dead and come down from heaven" (Lewis and Loomie 1953:89). The missionaries were still a few miles from their intended settlement at Ajacan. The natives promptly helped them move. The senior clerics remarked that the Algonquians performed a laborious task for them, carrying the clerics' goods "on their shoulders for 2 leagues" and then ferrying them an additional two and a half miles (Lewis and Loomie 1953:90–91).

The need to transport their goods suggested that the Jesuits' initial landing point off of the James River was unacceptable for settling. Segura and Quiros described the first area on which they unloaded their belongings as an uninhabited place (Lewis and Loomie 1953:90–91). The Jesuits did not want to be isolated from the natives; otherwise they would have likely accepted this tract of land that was free from current occupation. The missionaries' explicit purpose of proselytization required living in close proximity to the Ajacan Algonquians. The natives would be providing the Jesuits with daily sustenance, which was another reason for the clerics to live close to them.

After the Jesuit party had settled at Ajacan, the natives informed them that the three-year-old brother of Don Luis was in failing health. The novice asked one of the missionaries to baptize his brother (Lewis and Loomie 1953:89). Segura immediately dispatched a cleric for this task. The historical records did not mention whether the baptism was performed. A few days later, as the pilot of the Spanish vessel prepared to return to Mexico, he gave the clerics "half his supply of tar to patch up one of the [natives'] leaking canoes" (Lewis and Loomie 1953:91). None of the written accounts verified that the tar was given to the natives. Both the baptism and tar patch were potential gifts for the Algonquians.

In their status report to Spanish officials, Segura and Quiros pleaded for additional supplies. The Jesuits desired corn for both immediate consumption and future planting. Don Luis's previous boasts regarding the bounty of his homeland had led the missionaries to expect a local Chesapeake environment rich in food. To the contrary, the neophyte returned to a land "chastised . . . with six years of famine and death" (Lewis and Loomie 1953:89). Since the

European colonists depended on native food surpluses for subsistence and since indigenous crops wilted during drought conditions, these environmental pressures undoubtedly strained intercultural relations. Compounding matters, the journey to Ajacan had taken longer than expected and depleted the Jesuits' already "ill-provisioned" stores (Lewis and Loomie 1953:90). Accustomed to personal hardship, Segura and Quiros wrote that, "it seemed good to expose ourselves to th[e] risk" of starvation (Lewis and Loomie 1953:90). Segura, confident in apparently friendly relations with the natives, authorized the pilot and other nonreligious members of the Spanish crew to leave the Chesapeake despite his meager stores.

Don Luis continued to serve the Jesuits as a neophyte and translator after the pilot and other nonreligious crewmembers left the Chesapeake. Don Luis's service to the Jesuits and their primary purpose of missionization after the Spanish supply ship had left Ajacan strongly suggested that he did not journey to the Chesapeake for the sole purpose of killing the missionaries. The clerics promptly began their preliminary *entrada* proselytization phase, giving a few trinkets to the Ajacan natives, piquing their interest in Christianity, and beginning the conversion process. These gifts enabled the Jesuits to tell religious stories and explain ecclesiastical ideas to the natives. The clerics' sacred presents fulfilled the missionary-economy obligation of aiding in the conversion process. After a short period, however, Don Luis and the Ajacan natives abandoned the Jesuits, moving to the village of the neophyte's uncle. The impetus for the separation from the missionaries, who were dependent on the Ajacan natives for basic survival, can be better understood and justified through a review of exchange transactions between the two cultures.

A summary of the goods transacted during the second interaction period reflected a substantial exchange imbalance. The natives provided the missionaries with daily sustenance and services—extensive amounts of food and labor. Yet, the clerics' offerings were difficult to substantiate. They might have baptized an Algonquian youth, and they might have given the natives some tar to patch a canoe. Nevertheless, the historical records only verified the completion of one Jesuit offering to the indigenous population. Overall, in exchange for two months of daily meals, the Jesuits reciprocated their local benefactors with a couple of religious trinkets. The natives, however, failed to requite the missionaries for these trinkets. Every previous Spanish offering had been met with an Algonquian return gift, usually for sustenance. The lack of reciprocation by the natives suggested that they did not perceive the Spanish items as legitimate gifts or appropriate counter-gifts. This implied that the religious offerings failed to transfer or cancel debt. This substantial inadequacy in reciprocity likely explains why Don Luis and the other natives from Ajacan deserted these clerics.

At first, the Ajacan natives did not actively seek reciprocation. The "poor trade" between the anonymous Spanish crewman and one of the natives, however, revealed that the Europeans were capable of compensation. Since gift givers must be compensated within a limited time frame, the natives expected prompt Jesuit return offerings once the ability to compensate was revealed. Following that trade, the Algonquians began to make their desires for reciprocation explicit. They were now reluctant to give without a guarantee of a return offering. Marcel Mauss emphasized that presents of sustenance establish an especially important link between giver and recipient in gift economies. He concluded that, "the thing that is given forges a bilateral, irrevocable bond, above all when it consists of food" (Mauss 1990:59). In repeatedly offering food, which was supposed to produce the strongest of intercultural bonds and having witnessed the ability of the Spanish to relinquish goods that the natives desired during the "poor trade," the Chesapeake Algonquians anticipated either reciprocation from the clerics or their overwhelming indebtedness. They received neither. In gift-exchange terms, the clerics were slaves to the natives for offering insufficient tangible return gifts. According to Segura's missionary socioeconomics, however, the Jesuits owed the natives nothing. In presenting the unparalleled religious gift of eternal salvation, the missionaries felt that they merited the indigenous food offerings. These extremely different socioeconomic expectations, which constitute a very specific and distinct clash of cultural rules, contributed to the Ajacan Algonquians' decision to desert the missionaries.

Participants in gift-exchange systems equate refusing to give with a deliberate and insulting denial of partnership. In terms of the indigenous gift economy, the missionaries' absolute failure to reciprocate symbolized a rejection of the Ajacan natives. And even though the Algonquians privileged the bond between exchange partners over the equation of exchange values, material reciprocity was still required to maintain a gift-based relationship. The lack of countergifts dissolved the interpersonal ties that the initial gifts formed. Once it became apparent that the Jesuits were not going to reciprocate, the time limit for return gifts had elapsed, and the natives determined that they had been flagrantly denied by the clerics, they abandoned the Jesuits. From this moment on, the Ajacan natives and the Spanish Jesuits were aliens in two distinct ways; they lived far apart, and the Algonquians no longer offered legitimate gifts to the clerics. The interpersonal bonds established by gift exchange were severed. The missionaries' failure to reciprocate adequately pushed the Ajacan natives away from the Jesuits but did not necessitate any violent retribution. It merely terminated the alliance.

Many Chesapeake tribes kept seasonal villages (Williamson 2003:41). Floridian missionaries frequently experienced difficulties in converting nonsedentary indigenous populations because of their mobility (Bushnell 1990:475–490; 1981). The move by the Ajacan Algonquians to the interior could be interpreted as an effort to access a better hunting spot. Nevertheless, amicable relations between the Jesuits and Don Luis's tribe would have resulted in the groups moving to the interior together, or at least in Don Luis staying with the Jesuits. In addition, none of the historical records mentioned that this was a seasonal move for the natives, and all of them emphasized that Don Luis and his Algonquian followers deliberately and maliciously deserted the clerics.

The historical records gave conflicting accounts regarding how long Don Luis stayed with the missionaries before leading the native abandonment. Rogel's two accounts and Martinez's relation asserted that Don Luis left Ajacan about a week after the Spanish ship left the Chesapeake (Lewis and Loomie 1953:109). Sacchini pushed the neophyte's departure forward two weeks and described a gradual frustration that Don Luis experienced with the missionaries. The disappointment and rejection that participants in a gift economy experience while waiting for the time limit on expected reciprocity to expire would gradually grow until the alliance was entirely dissolved.

Segura had relied on the expectation that Don Luis would mediate any conflicts between the Ajacan missionaries and Chesapeake Algonquians. However, Don Luis's previous experiences in La Florida and past interaction with elite Europeans had not prepared him for these specific socioeconomic misunderstandings. Segura's no-trade policy with intended converts grew out of his recent tour of unsuccessful Floridian missions. His rules, designed to prevent further failure, were distinct from what Don Luis had witnessed in other missions in La Florida. Furthermore, the neophyte had not experienced the reciprocal inequities on display at Ajacan when interacting with King Philip II and Admiral Menéndez. Each of his exchanges with them had been balanced. Therefore, Don Luis would have been hard-pressed to anticipate or solve the weighty socioeconomic discrepancies confronting Segura and his Ajacan crew.

## Period III: Abandonment

Isolated and alienated from the natives who had formerly procured their daily means, the Jesuits needed a new way to acquire food. Rogel remarked that the missionaries "got along as best they could, going to other villages to barter for maize with copper and tin" (Lewis and Loomie 1953:109). This type of transaction differed significantly from the previous sequence of gift exchanges. Rogel's use of the word "barter," like Quiros's emphasis on "poor trade," revealed that these transactions included the immediate transfer of something for something. The exchanges were between individuals of unknown rank who had never transacted before and might not transact again. These transfers of European copper and tin for native maize marked the first instances of commodity exchange between the Jesuits and the neighboring Algonquians since the "poor trade" that so angered Segura. The missionaries needed food from the neighboring Algonquian villages and favored the utility of the material items over the bond between exchange partners. They were oblivious to the effects that these transactions would likely have on their relationships with previous exchange partners, namely Don Luis's tribe. Segura's injunction against trade with natives that he intended to convert did not apply to these transactions because the neighboring Algonquians fell outside of the intended proselytization area. Rogel specified that the missionaries traded with Algonquians from "other villages" (Lewis and Loomie 1953:158). The missionaries had no previous contact with these other villages and dealt with them only for food.

Rogel indirectly described a second instance of the Jesuits seeking trade with the neighboring Algonquians. He wrote that, "[Segura] decided to send Father Quiros and Brother Gabriel de Solis and Brother Juan Baptista to the village of the chief near where Don Luis was staying. Thus they could take Don Luis along with them and *barter for maize on the way back*" (Italics added; Lewis and Loomie 1953:109–110). Quiros and his team had two distinct goals for their visit to the village led by Don Luis's uncle: to reacquire the neophyte, and to barter for maize on the way back with the neighboring Algonquians. These tasks were separate and involved two distinct groups of natives, each with a different exchange or trade status. The first involved Algonquians associated with Don Luis, formerly of Ajacan. The second involved another Algonquian group that could be engaged in trade, as they were not the targets for proselytization. These other Algonquians, however, were rivals to the native inhabitants of Ajacan.

Later actions by Don Luis indicated that he and the others residing at his uncle's village had food to spare. This contradicted any notion that Segura did not trade with the former Ajacan natives because he thought they had no surplus. During the first week of February 1571, Don Luis made two additional offerings of nourishment to the missionaries. In neither case did the gifts surprise the Jesuits. They acted as if they knew these natives were moderately well stocked. Furthermore, the historical records did not describe a food shortage at the village of Don Luis's uncle. Quiros and his associates never attempted to trade with the former Ajacan natives. On the contrary, the missionaries asked for a handout of food from them. Until the moment they were murdered, the Jesuits maintained a division between exclusive gift exchange with the former Ajacan natives they intended to convert, and commodity exchange with the neighboring Algonquian tribe(s) they did not plan to proselytize. Frederic Gleach emphasized an additional flaw in the argument that the Algonquians killed the Jesuits because of the demands the Europeans [and the drought] placed on the indigenous food surplus. He noted that, "We see in later chapters that the Indians in Virginia possessed sufficient stores of food in the early seventeenth century to survive considerable deprivation, and there is no reason to assure that this represented any change from their sixteenth-century way of living" (Gleach 1997:90–91). Martin Gallivan's archaeological investigations also highlighted the burgeoning storage capacity of Chesapeake Algonquian villages during this time (Gallivan 2003, 2004).

In their burgeoning competitive tribute system, Chesapeake Algonquians passed prized goods, especially items of European origin, to their weroances and perhaps to a prototype Mamanatowick. They gained prestige through the offerings and competed with fellow Algonquians for status. Exchange relations controlled and reflected the social hierarchy. Thus, after refusing to requite them or trade with them, the Jesuits further insulted Don Luis and the members of his tribe by trading with rival Algonquian groups. By providing the neighboring rivals with prestigious goods, while failing to do so with the Ajacan natives, they humiliated Don Luis and his followers. Doing so would prove to be deadly to this Jesuit mission, as understood posthumously by Jamestown's John Smith. He affirmed that Chesapeake Algonquians overwhelmingly dreaded public embarrassment and avenged it with the blood of individuals who had disgraced them. He wrote that these natives "seldome make warrs for landes or goodes, but . . . principally for revendge, so vindictiue they be, to be made derision of, and to be insulted" (Smith et al. 1986, 1:165).

Mauss's model of the gift economy equated failure to reciprocate with a loss of status, freedom, and spiritual essence (Mauss 1990:39). Under these guidelines, the missionaries were socially dead creatures. The former Ajacan natives had provided them with the gift of life—repeated sustenance—which had not been requited. From the Algonquian viewpoint, the Jesuits' had owed the Ajacan natives everything, including their lives and souls. However, through an additional gift-economy violation, trade with a rival Algonquian tribe, these social corpses managed to further offend Don Luis and his tribal members. The missionaries supplied the rivals of Don Luis and his followers with prestigious items that would be passed up the indigenous hierarchy in exchange for status. Even though the former Ajacan natives had intentionally distanced themselves from the Jesuits, they found themselves again socially diminished by the clerics.

The trade between the Jesuits and the neighboring rivals of the former Ajacan natives likely upset Don Luis. But the ultimate missionary insult occurred when Quiros visited and asked Don Luis to help the clerics in these socially degrading trades. In essence, they requested that the neophyte assist them in further humiliating himself and his people. Even if the former Ajacan natives had not heard of how the Jesuits had engaged their rivals and even if they had attempted to ignore this social affront, the Jesuits made their past exchange violations obvious, unavoidable, and undeniable by publicly asking Don Luis to help them additionally dishonor his fellow Algonquians. Following one social offense and on the verge of further public embarrassment, the natives struck back.

### Period IV: Algonquian Attacks

As instructed, Quiros and the two other Jesuits went to the village where Don Luis and his followers now resided. Quiros asked the novice to rejoin the missionaries and to help them trade with neighboring Algonquians on the way back to Ajacan. Don Luis responded by offering the missionaries a small gift of food. The offer of grain from the former Ajacan natives to the missionaries appeared to be a gift, considering its something-for-nothing form and that it occurred between individuals who had previously transacted. Much to the contrary, this intentionally one-sided transaction confirmed the imbalance in the native/missionary relations. Don Luis used this duplicitous transaction to punctuate the impending death of the clerics.

The Algonquians could have easily slaughtered the Jesuits without such trickery as a false offering. The missionaries had no weapons. However, Don Luis intentionally deceived Quiros. The Jesuits had inadvertently denied an alliance with the Ajacan natives by accepting food without properly reciprocating. The missionaries were symbolically led to their execution with a duplicitous offering of sustenance as the result of repeated gift-economy violations. These three Jesuits, whose lives had been maintained by Algonquian gifts of food, died while accepting a final native handout of sustenance. Sacchini wrote that Don "Luis pierced the heart of Quiros with an arrow" while "the other [natives] killed his two companions" (Lewis and Loomie 1953:223). Don Luis and a group of Algonquians then traveled to Ajacan to inflict revenge on the remaining Jesuits.

As with the murder of Quiros and his two comrades, Don Luis and his fellow native Algonquians formerly of Ajacan chose to eliminate the clerics with particular symbolism. They disguised their lethal intentions with a false gift. The neophyte and his fellow natives "asked [the clerics] for hatchets and other tools . . . in order to construct a church" for Segura (Lewis and Loomie 1953:181).

The Jesuits promptly gave them the tools. This transaction seemed to be a gift, consisting of exchange partners who had interacted before and would apparently interact again. It appeared to re-establish and repair interpersonal bonds. The ulterior motive of Don Luis and his followers, however, dictated that this exchange was far from a benevolent something-for-nothing offering. Don Luis drew blood first, striking Segura with the "hatchets which . . . [the Jesuits] brought along for trading" (Lewis and Loomie 1953:110, 182). The neophyte's native companions then finished off the four remaining missionaries (Lewis and Loomie 1953:110). During the week that followed the Algonquian annihilation of the clerics, Don Luis and the former Ajacan natives stole and redistributed the goods of the deceased missionaries.

Iron hatchets figured prominently in the story of the Chesapeake Jesuits. The Ajacan natives greatly desired these goods because they would have allowed them to gain status with indigenous leaders via a tribute offering. The natives transported the hatchets, along with the rest of the Jesuits' belongings, as part of a laborious task that went unrewarded. In addition, the Ajacan natives provided daily sustenance for the missionaries. Yet, the clerics never reciprocated by offering goods, especially the hatchets, to the Ajacan natives. To the Algonquians, the missionaries' failure to part with these tools was a refusal of alliance. It resulted in the clerics' abandonment by the natives. The final insult occurred when the clerics traded the hatchets to the neighboring rivals of the former Ajacan locals. This humiliation of Don Luis and his native kin incited them to strike. The former Ajacan Algonquians purposefully elected to punish the Jesuits for their exchange violations with the hatchets. Overall, the missionaries incited the Algonquians to strike by transgressing the native gift-exchange system and were slaughtered with the exact items that they refused to give. Don Luis and his followers responded to the Jesuits' socioeconomic violations with reciprocal vengeance (Mitchell 1997:15).

*Period V: Spanish Retribution*

Two weeks after Don Luis had slaughtered the Jesuits, King Philip II granted the supplies the missionaries had previously requested. Captain Vicente Gonzales and Brother Juan Salcedo led a supply ship to Ajacan in the spring of 1571. Gonzales and his crew sailed into the Chesapeake Bay and up the James River. The Spanish captain saw many Algonquians dressed in the missionaries' garments encouraging his crew to come ashore. Gonzales did not trust the odd yet seemingly friendly behavior of the natives. He anchored but let the Algonquians come to him. When a group of natives paddled out to the Spanish vessel, the captain and his men seized two of them.

The indigenous prisoners informed their captors of the Jesuits' demise. When the Spanish captain and crew returned to Havana and told Menéndez of the missionaries' deaths, the admiral planned an immediate retaliatory trip. Although the Spanish could not be certain of Segura's death, they feared the worst. After a series of delays, the Spanish revisited the Chesapeake in August of 1572. Led by Menéndez himself, the crew consisted of Father Rogel, Captain Gonzales, and thirty soldiers and sailors. Their mission had two objectives: to reacquire Alonso de Olmos from the natives, and to punish the Algonquians responsible for the murder of the Ajacan Jesuits. The admiral believed that Don Luis's politically powerful relatives had forced the neophyte to attack Segura and his followers. Consequently, Menéndez wanted to capture Don Luis's uncle most of all.

As soon as they arrived in the Chesapeake, the Spanish set their plan in motion. The admiral surveyed the indigenous population by encouraging natives to come aboard his vessel and receive goods. Menéndez baited the Algonquians with gifts of "honey-cakes and biscuits," which the natives eagerly accepted (Lewis and Loomie 1953:184). The admiral used a simple criterion for determining indigenous guilt, equating culpability in the slaughter of the Ajacan missionaries with individuals that currently wore the cleric's religious items. Natives adorned with ecclesiastical goods that boarded the ship to accept Spanish gifts walked straight into Menéndez's trap. One Algonquian "wore as a decoration . . . a silver paten [a metal plate that holds the wafer during Communion]"; other natives "covered their private parts with the corporals [altar cloth]" (Lewis and Loomie 1953:108, 184).

Gleach believed that the Algonquian wearing of slain missionary goods indicated that "the Indians . . . recognized the power of these items and wore them with respect" (Gleach 1997:96). On the contrary, it is argued here that the Algonquians wore the Jesuit items as symbols of conquest. Using the altar cloth as a loincloth is hardly a sign of respect. These goods and the way they were displayed showcased native independence, dominance, and retribution. John Smith reported that early 17th-century Chesapeake Algonquians frequently decorated themselves with trophies from their victims (Smith et al. 1986, 1:161). The wearing of enemy goods most likely symbolized conflict and conquest, not acculturation and reverence for another group's religious beliefs.

Regardless of the meaning behind the use of these items, the Spanish seized the individuals wearing the clerical goods. The Admiral's plan worked; his crew captured the uncle of Don Luis in the ambush. In the process of taking captives, the Spanish killed 20 natives. Having succeeded in the initial objective of his plan, Menéndez turned his attention toward the second goal. The admiral made inquiries regarding the status and location of Alonso de Olmos. A group of Algonquians informed him that a chief in the interior currently detained Olmos. Rogel believed that Menéndez intended to offer the native hostages in exchange for Olmos. The admiral, however, had other plans. He sent trinkets to the chief who held the boy in an attempt to obtain Olmos without relinquishing his captives. Menéndez's offering was the first gift exchange between Spanish colonists and Chesapeake Algonquians since the Ajacan natives had abandoned the Jesuits in the fall of 1570. It established an interpersonal bond between the two groups that both sides were eager to sustain. The Spanish offered the gift in hopes of securing a safe return for Olmos. Likewise, the natives accepted the present in an attempt at ensuring the release of the hostages that the Admiral held. Rogel noted that, "as soon as the chief learned of the capture of other [Algonquians] . . . he sought to curry favor with Governor [Menéndez]" (Lewis and Loomie 1953:109.

The group of natives holding Olmos immediately returned him to the Spanish. Even though the boy was safely in his custody, the Admiral did not relinquish his captives. Two factors intensified Menéndez's wrath: (1) Olmos's testimony regarding the murder of the Jesuits, and (2) an Algonquian attempt at freeing the captured chiefs. Menéndez now held Don Luis responsible for Segura's slaughter. On the basis of the new information from Olmos, the admiral made a deal with his hostages. Menéndez insisted that Don Luis's uncle "bring in Don Luis . . . for punishment, and if he did not do this, the Governor would punish all those captured" (Lewis and Loomie 1953:110). Menéndez offered the native chief a temporary stay of execution for himself and the captives in exchange for the neophyte. The chief agreed and promised to return with his nephew in five days or less. When a week passed and Don Luis's uncle neither handed over his nephew nor returned to the admiral's ship, Menéndez ordered the execution of the hostages. Before hanging them from the ship's yardarms, Rogel baptized the captives.

Menéndez's manipulations of the indigenous gift-exchange system enabled him to accomplish strikingly different goals without enduring a single Spanish casualty. Attempting to reacquire Olmos and simultaneously punish the Algonquians responsible for the Ajacan slaughter necessitated careful management of native economic expectations. The admiral's false offerings of "honey-cakes and biscuits" served to screen the indigenous population and locate elite Algonquians who had had a hand in Segura's murder. Once Menéndez had acquired Don Luis's uncle he could have simply engineered a hostage trade for Olmos. This exchange, however, would have forced him to abandon the second of his two goals. He wanted to punish the natives. Instead of attempting to

Table 3.1. Ajacan exchange and violence

| Date | Exchange Number | Exchange Type | Exchange-system violation | Consequences |
|------|----------------|---------------|---------------------------|--------------|
| 1565 | 1 | Gift | | |
| | 2 | Commodity | | |
| | 3 | Gift | | |
| 1566 | 4 | Other | | |
| 1570 | 5–7 | Gift | | |
| | 8 | Commodity | 1. Nonreligious exchange with intended converts; violates missionary economy | 1a. Segura prohibits future nonreligious exchange with potential converts<br>1b. Natives expect reciprocation |
| | 9–10 | Gift | | |
| | 11–12 | Other | | |
| | 13 | Gift | 2. Failure to reciprocate; violates gift system and is a refusal of alliance | 2. Natives desert Jesuits |
| 1571 | 14 | Commodity | 3. Exchange with tribute rivals after failure to reciprocate; violates gift system by socially privileging rivals and diminishing former partners | 3. Natives attack Jesuits (murder in exchanges 17 and 20, violence is continued in exchanges 22, 24, and 30) |
| | 15–25 | Other or Violence | | |
| 1572 | 26–27 | Gift | | |
| | 28–31 | Other or Violence | | |

exchange captives, the admiral offered trinkets to the native chief holding Olmos. He encouraged reciprocation through his gift and created a false sense of good will. Although Olmos's return merited a reciprocal offering from the Spanish, Menéndez ignored the debt he owed the Algonquian leader. Olmos's testimony revealed that the admiral was no closer to fulfilling his second goal than when he entered the Chesapeake. Don Luis was responsible for the Jesuit deaths, not his uncle. Menéndez, having already used false gifts and genuine gifts to his advantage, attempted to acquire the neophyte through commodity exchange. He tried to trade Don Luis's uncle for Don Luis, but the native chief did not honor the agreement. The admiral witnessed firsthand that the indigenous population could be successfully manipulated through gift exchange; trade, however, was a far less effective method of control. Ex-neophytes frequently became formidable resistance leaders. Their knowledge of colonial tactics made them particularly savvy in intercultural strife (Lightfoot 2005:90; Phillips 1975; Holterman 1970a, 1970b). Thus, it is not surprising that Don Luis avoided Menéndez's trap.

Despite the unsuccessful results of missionization at Ajacan, Jesuit ventures at native spiritual conversion succeeded elsewhere, especially outside of La Florida (Polzer 1976; Thomas 1990; Codignola 1995:203; Milanich 1999:99). Missionary and gift economies did not always oppose each other, and their followers were not destined for inevitable conflict. Unique factors distinguished the Ajacan undertaking from other attempts at European settlement. Segura's frustration with jaded missionaries throughout La Florida made him especially idealistic and strict in terms of economic interaction with the natives. His interpretation of the missionary economy was extreme, as was his decision to prevent experienced clerics or soldiers from joining the Ajacan crew. The individuality of separate Chesapeake Algonquian tribes, their intense competition within the burgeoning chiefdom-wide tribute system, and the fierce Chesapeake Algonquian hatred of social embarrassment were additional elements that made this contact situation unique. The exact sequence of exchange violations also contributed to the singularity of Ajacan (Table 3.1). For instance, the initial "poor trade" implied to the natives that the Jesuits possessed the ability to trade with their indigenous benefactors and thus exaggerated the clerics' later failure to reciprocate. Overall, these unique aspects of the Ajacan mission intensified the Jesuits' socioeconomic transgressions of the Algonquian gift-exchange system and ultimately led, at least in part, to the demise of Segura and his followers.

# 4
# *Roanoke*

The first English attempts at settling North America occurred in Carolina Algonquian territory during the 1580s. Neither the 1584 precolony venture nor the three subsequent colonies resulted in permanent English settlement. The local Ossomocomuck Algonquian tribes that the English engaged maintained separate identities and frequently antagonized one another. Unlike European/ Algonquian interaction at Ajacan, Ossomocomuck reactions to gift-exchange violations by the English were more influenced by opportunities to gain power within Carolina territory than with the specific transgressions of the colonists. Natives manipulated exchange practices, unsuspecting English settlers, and tribal alliances in their struggles with one another. These actions were consistent with Algonquian notions of justice, equilibrium, and reciprocity, yet also revealed the political factors that could override expected indigenous punishments from various socioeconomic transgressions.

## The History

English/Carolina Algonquian interaction can be divided into the following six periods:

(1) Precolony ventures
(2) Lane's First Colony—initial interaction from July 1585 to March 1586
(3) Lane's First Colony—Chawanoac trip during March and April of 1586
(4) Lane's First Colony—last months of settlement from April to June 1586
(5) Grenville's Second Colony—August 1586
(6) White's Third Colony—1587 to 1590

*Period I: Precolony Ventures*

More than 100 miles to the south of Ajacan and 50 years before Segura's demise, Italian explorer Giovanni da Verrazzano visited the Outer Banks, a chain of islands off of present-day North Carolina. His landing and search of the immediate area in 1524 resulted in the first historically documented European contact with the indigenous population of the Carolinas (Perdue 1985:61). The initial English attempt at permanent settlement in this region did not occur for another 60 years. Sir Walter Raleigh received an official patent for North American colonization from England's Queen Elizabeth I on March 25, 1584 (Quinn 1984:9). Raleigh's franchise on establishing English possessions in the Americas included any territory without Christian inhabitants.

As a result of repeated international aggressions, settlements along the southeastern coast of North America transformed from relatively simple colonial ventures into strategic military loci for naval repair and refurbishment. There was substantial booty in almost every vessel leaving the mineral rich lands adjacent to the Caribbean Sea and Gulf of Mexico, destined for Europe. To protect this material wealth, Spanish and English governments attempted to keep confidential the location of their American colonies. England's interests in the Americas coincided with its desire to attack Spain's seemingly inexhaustible source of material wealth in the West Indies (Kupperman 1984:13). Spanish claims to North America extended along the eastern coast of La Florida to a vague northern border that included the Chesapeake. Missionary attempts at colonizing Ajacan, a village north of the 37th north parallel, in 1566 and 1570–71 demonstrated Spain's perceived rights to the Middle Atlantic. Although England recognized a significantly smaller La Florida region, Raleigh avoided an international confrontation by making discreet plans to establish an English colony near the Outer Banks (Kupperman 1984:5). In not announcing their intentions to the Spanish, the English managed to plant a semicovert settlement well south of Segura's failed mission.

Raleigh provided financial backing for two English ships that set sail for the Americas in April of 1584. The Queen maintained a vested interest in the potential English colony because it affected the European balance of power. Although not officially at war with each other until 1585, Spain and England preyed upon each other's American ships throughout the early 1580s (Quinn 1984:53). The Queen forbade Raleigh from traveling to America himself on the trip and on many of the journeys that followed. In his place, Raleigh chose Philip Amadas and Arthur Barlowe to lead a small crew to the Carolinas for the 1584 precolony venture. Raleigh instructed Amadas and Barlowe to search the territory north of Spain's La Florida and establish amicable relations with the indigenous population.

Anchored off of Roanoke Island during the initial Carolina scouting mission by the English, Amadas, Barlowe, and their European crew spied a boat with three natives in it approaching them on July 16, 1584. The Algonquians landed on the shore near the English vessel and one of them paced back and forth along the adjacent beach. Amadas, Barlowe, and the pilot Simao Fernandes decided to attempt communication with the native. They boarded their pinnace and rowed to where the Algonquian stood. The native said many things to the Europeans, none of which they understood. Amadas and his associates responded by offering him clothing and food. After receiving the English goods, the native set out to obtain return offerings for his new acquaintances. He began to fish and before long had caught more than enough food to reward the Europeans for their generosity. Barlowe reported that the Algonquian "diuided his fishe [his total catch] into two partes, pointing one part to the shippe [for the English], and the other to the Pinnesse [for himself].., requit[ing] the former benefits receaued" (Quinn 1955:98). Barlowe's use of the word "requite" implied that the English perceived the native gift as reciprocation for their initial offerings.

The following day Roanoac Chief Granganimeo led 50 men to the shore alongside the English vessel. His servants placed a long reed mat on the ground for the weroance and four other high-ranking Roanoacs. These native leaders sat on the woven covering; the rest of the Algonquian group stood off at each side. As the English explorers approached Granganimeo, the chief made "all signes of joy, and welcome" (Quinn 1955:99). He then gave a lengthy monologue, the content of which again went unappreciated by the Europeans. When the speech ended, Barlowe gave Granganimeo many presents. The English made similar offerings to the lesser weroances sitting beside the Roanoac leader. However, Granganimeo intercepted these goods and explained to the explorers that, "all things ought to be deliuered vnto him [because] the rest [of the natives present] were but his seruants, and followers" (Quinn 1955:100). Although Amadas and Barlowe intended to present the others with gifts, they wound up making another offering to the head weroance. Granganimeo strictly enforced the rules of the native gift exchange, demanding that this transaction engage individuals of equivalent status and not include any of his subordinates.

Unlike Barlowe's narrative, which described the initial amicable relations, the anonymous manuscript associated with John White's 1585–86 drawings provided a different description of the first interaction between the English and Roanoacs. It reported that the Europeans' arrival stunned the indigenous population, causing them to "make a great and horrible crye . . . like wild beasts or men out of their wyts" (Quinn 1955:414). The English calmed the natives by offering them many small presents. Upon receiving these gifts, the Roanoacs led them to a nearby town where Granganimeo and his men entertained them. Although Barlowe's discourse and the White/Harriot narrative gave strikingly dissimilar details of first contact, they both described a common pattern of events: initial gift giving by the English led to immediate native reciprocation. Barlowe's report was limited to a discussion of the precolony venture in the summer of 1584. The White/Harriot narrative described a jumble of events from the middle 1580s and might have referred to English/Carolina Algonquian interaction during 1585 instead of the 1584 venture described by Barlowe.

During the five weeks in the summer of 1584 when the English resided in and around Roanoke Island, Granganimeo sustained them with daily gifts of food. Amadas and Barlowe regularly requited the weroance and bartered with lesser-ranking natives. On July 18 or 19, 1584, the English traded with the Roanoacs, exchanging European tin and copper to the Algonquians for animal skins (Quinn 1955:100–101). A few days later, Amadas and Barlowe invited Granganimeo aboard their vessel, where the Roanoac weroance was introduced to English cuisine, including wine, meat, and bread (Quinn 1955:101). The English then exchanged with natives from all over the region who had come to Roanoke (Quinn 1955:103). Later that week, Granganimeo's wife served an elaborate meal to the English crew at her village. Before the Roanoacs fed Amadas and his colleagues, the chief's spouse had her servants wash the clothes and feet of the visitors. Before leaving the North American Middle Atlantic, the Europeans briefly surveyed areas to the west and north and entered the Chesapeake Bay. Amadas, Barlowe, and their crew left Roanoke Island for England in September of 1584 and retained two natives, named Manteo and Wanchese. In hopes of strengthening communication, the Europeans and Algonquians intended to increase their proficiency in the other's language during the trip and the natives' stay in England. Historical writers, like Raphael Holinshed, Diego Hernández de Quinones, and Hernando de Altamirano, verified the Algonquians' stay in England. Overall, during the 1584 precolony venture, the European explorers maintained amicable relations with the indigenous population by offering gifts to elite Algonquians, engaging the others in trade, and effectively reciprocating with the natives in a timely manner.

Bolstered by the success of Amadas and Barlowe's voyage to Roanoke Island,

Raleigh prepared a second venture to the Carolinas. The Reverend Richard Hakluyt, an Oxford trained minister who studied and wrote extensively on colonization during the 1580s, maintained a close friendship with Raleigh and significantly influenced his preparations for England's first attempt at settling the Americas (Noël Hume 1994:28; Armitage 1995:52–75). Both the Reverend Hakluyt and his uncle, also named Richard, distinguished English colonization plans from contemporaneous Spanish endeavors in terms of the allegedly different ways the rival Europeans treated the indigenous population. They maintained that Spain dominated her colonies with "barbarous cruelty," as opposed to English settlers who treated Carolina natives "with all humanitie, curtesie, and freedome" (Kupperman 1984:32; Quinn 1955:138). The *Anonymous Notes for the Guidance of Ralegh and Cavendish [on their First Colony venture]*, written in 1584 and 1585, echoed the Hakluyts' ideas on colonialism. These formal instructions listed rules concerning frontier behavior, including: "[Rule] 6 That non shall stryke or mysuse any Indian, [and Rule] 7 That non shall Enter any Indians howse without his leaue" (Quinn 1955:138). Punishments for violating these regulations entailed: "[For Rule] 6, to have xx [20] blows with a cuggell [a short club] in the presetz of the Indian strucken. To [Rule] .7. vj [six] monthes imprisonment or slauery" (Quinn 1955:139). Although neither Amadas nor Barlowe broke these rules during their visit to the Carolinas in 1584, many English colonists would be unable to make similar claims during future ventures at Roanoke Island.

Backed by Raleigh and the Crown, 1,000 colonists left Plymouth, England, on seven ships in April of 1585 for North America. During the transatlantic voyage, severe storms scattered the vessels and destroyed one of the pinnaces. The *Tiger*, captained by Raleigh's cousin General Richard Grenville, landed at Puerto Rico in early May of 1585. Captain Thomas Cavendish and the *Elizabeth* joined them a week later. The tumultuous voyage to the Americas had severely depleted both the *Tiger's* and *Elizabeth's* supplies. When setting up camp in Puerto Rico, Grenville's men encountered some local Spanish patrolmen. The two groups arranged a future exchange for food, but the Spanish sentries did not come to the designated trading place at the appointed time. Their decision to avoid exchange infuriated Grenville, who burned the woods surrounding the Spaniards' camp as punishment. This was a common European practice to retaliate with an over-abundance of force to prevent other colonists or indigenous populations from perceiving the English as either feeble or forgiving (Quinn 1955:67). Pyrotechnic practices of this sort started under King Richard II during the 14th century and flourished during Queen Elizabeth I's subjugation of Irish and North American natives 200 years later (Jennings 1975:153).

English soldiers also refined this technique when serving with other Protestant forces in the Low Countries during this time (Webb 1979).

*Period II: First Colony—Initial Interaction (July 1585–March 1586)*

Grenville and the crew of the *Tiger* arrived in the Carolinas in the middle of July 1585. The ship's anonymous journal recorded accounts of the crew's initial interactions with Carolina natives. According to this document, they first sailed to the Secotan town of Aquascococke. The only entry recorded was that of a purported theft of a silver cup by a native from the English. The journal gave few details of the theft, referring to the event simply as a reason for Grenville to return to this village three days later. In between the alleged theft and the rendezvous for its planned return, the crew of the *Tiger* visited the nearby village of Secotan and "were well intertayned there [by] the Sauages" (Quinn 1955:191). Grenville and his men then returned to Aquascococke to receive the stolen cup that the natives had promised to return, but the Algonquians did not produce the item in question.

In stealing the cup, pledging to return it, and then reneging, the Secotans committed two commodity-exchange violations: theft and a broken contract. Both of these economic affronts resulted in the English receiving no compensation for the cup. Avenging both of these commodity-exchange transgressions, Grenville and his men "burnt, and spoyled their corne, and Towne" (Quinn 1955:191).

The lack of details provided in the anonymous ship's journal regarding this incident of native theft followed by destructive English retribution undermines the viability of any historical interpretation. Yet, it still leaves the reader with the unanswered questions of why the natives took the silver cup from the English in the first place and why they did not return it later as promised. Using events and historical records from other settlements, it is plausible to interpret the events leading up to the English assault as an exchange-based cultural conflict. The journal entry stated that other Secotan villages entertained the crew after the initial theft at Aquascococke and before the expected return of the item. There is no mention, however, of the crew reciprocating the generosity shown by these natives. The English likely perceived the indigenous gifts—entertainment and food—as something for nothing. Conversely, the Carolina Algonquians considered their presents as offerings that would be repaid in a later exchange. Without proper compensation by the colonists, the Algonquians took the cup for themselves, an act the settlers perceived as theft. Thus, each cultural group considered itself slighted by the other, according to their respective economic systems. Multiple examples of indigenous theft following settler refusals to reciprocate exist in the historical records from this time period, including a strikingly parallel incident at the Jamestown colony in 1607 that is discussed in the following chapter.

But why did the natives refuse to return the silver cup after they had taken it? Under the rules of gift exchange, the act of returning the object would dissolve the interpersonal bond and symbolic alliance between the Secotan Algonquians and the colonists. On the contrary, commodity economics mandated that only the immediate return of the cup would prevent hostilities. Misunderstanding and violence resulted because the two cultures maintained exclusive perspectives on the issues of gift giving, alliance, and reciprocation.

Four of the English vessels, the *Tiger, Elizabeth, Lion,* and *Dorothy,* reunited at their planned destination in the Carolinas two weeks later on July 27, 1585. With few spoiled supplies, the English split their crew. Led by Governor Ralph Lane, 100 colonists stayed at Roanoke Island. The others returned to England in August of 1585. Lane and his men constituted the First Colony. They promptly constructed fortifications, deemed Fort Ralegh. Trade flourished between the Europeans and natives, with English metals and trifles being traded for Roanoac food, animal skins, and pearls (Quinn 1955:331, 371, 333, 837). The burning of the Secotans' Aquascococke village had no apparent detrimental effects on English/Roanoac interaction. The historical records detailed no gift giving between the settlers and the Roanoacs during this period, suggesting that the relationships between these groups had changed. Whereas gifts comprised three-quarters of the Period I (precolony venture of 1584) English/Roanoac transactions, the second period (initial interaction of the 1st colony in late 1585/early 1586) contained no gift giving. This transformation indicated a shift in exchange focus, switching from an emphasis on the interpersonal bonds between exchange partners to the identities of the goods transacted. It also intimated a gradual alienation of two groups that had forsaken the ceremony of gift exchange for the immediate material profits of trade.

European diseases, likely measles or smallpox, began to decimate native towns that had been visited by the colonists. The indigenous population had never encountered the illnesses they now faced. Thomas Harriot observed that the epidemic first struck those areas where the English had experienced troubles, reporting that, "There was no towne where wee had any subtile deuise practised against vs [by the natives] . . . that within a few dayes after our departure . . . the people began to die very fast" (Quinn 1955:378).

Determining the identity of the specific Algonquian tribe is important because of consequent retribution and alliances that stemmed from the epidemic. Three lines of evidence suggested that the first Ossomocomuck group to be infected by English diseases was the Secotans. First, although the historical records included no instances of the Algonquians mentioning illness following the precolony venture in 1584, they contained explicit references regarding the immediate impact of the epidemic on the natives following English encounters in 1585. The initial Algonquian group contacted by the English carrying the contagion would likely be the first group infected. Historical records affirmed that Grenville and his men interacted with the Secotans before any other natives. Second, Harriot's narrative indicated that Roanoac enemies felt the effects of English maladies before other tribes. The Secotans and the Roanoacs were bitter adversaries during this time. Chief Wingina of the Roanoacs had been "shotte in two places through the bodye, and once cleane through the thigh" a year earlier by the Secotans who "maintaine[d] a deadlie and terrible warre" with the Roanoacs (Quinn 1955:101). Third, Harriot asserted that natives who "had dealt ill with" the colonists were the first to fall victim to the epidemic (Quinn 1955:379). The historical records indicated that Roanoac "enemies had abused" the English (Quinn 1955:378). The only documented First Colony altercation up to the outbreak of the European diseases was the dispute between the settlers and Secotan Aquascocockians over the silver cup. The theft and broken promise was the only recorded example of a negative incident between these groups that could be characterized as a "subtle device practiced against" the English. Overall, the Secotans were the only tribe that fit the descriptions of the native group that first suffered from the epidemic.

Since Algonquians who antagonized the English were the first to suffer from Western ailments, the indigenous population concluded that the colonists and their deity controlled the maladies. They believed that the settlers could direct their diseases to strike Algonquians who had wronged them. Harriot noted that, "[the natives] were perswaded that it [the epidemic] was the worke of our God through our meanes, and that wee by him might kil and slaie who wee would without weapons and not come neere them" (Quinn 1955:378). Although neither the colonists nor the natives understood the ways in which pathogens were exchanged, the indigenous population nonetheless perceived this epidemic as the result of powerful English forces. In Algonquian eyes, inflicting a disease on an individual was a deliberately hostile action. The settlers never identified the epidemic in their narratives nor explicitly accepted responsibility for it. They did, however, recognize that native devastation followed each of their visits. European contagions eventually infected many Roanoacs as well. As the diseases spread, Wingina repeatedly begged the English to ask their deity for mercy.

Of course, the English did not have the power to reverse the course of disease as requested. Yet, the Roanoacs saw the epidemic as intentional English antagonism, especially after witnessing how the colonists had seemingly punished the Secotans for their malice. This appearance of hostility undermined the alliances established between the settlers and Roanoacs two years earlier. The perception of aggression in combination with seeming refusal to divert the diseases further denied the union that these groups once had. Thus, the Algonquians believed that the epidemic demanded retribution. Indigenous justice emphasized the maintenance of equilibrium (Kupperman 1984:51). The inhabitants of Ossomocomuck followed a practice of retaliating in kind, avenging their own casualties with the lives of the individuals who were responsible. The Roanoac weroance survived the winter of 1585, but his brother Granganimeo and many others did not. With the passing of his sibling, Chief Wingina changed his name to Pemisipan. Pemisipan was likely Wingina's war name, a title used once he had decided to annihilate the First Colony (Kupperman 1984:76). Enraged by the overall effects of the diseases, the death of his brother, and the flagrant denial of alliance by the English, Pemisipan now began to plot the downfall of the colonists.

Granganimeo had been a close friend of the English and their highest-ranking native ally. He had orchestrated many gift exchanges during the 1584 precolony visit. With his death the settlers lost a strong interpersonal and intercultural bond. Granganimeo's demise undermined relations for two reasons: it undermined the indigenous gift economy and it removed a key liaison. This loss, an additional consequence of devastating European illnesses that devoured many native lives, crippled English relations with the Roanoacs. It further alienated the two parties and prompted immediate indigenous hostility.

*Period III: First Colony—the Chawanoac Trip (March/April 1586)*

By March of 1586, deteriorating relations with the Roanoacs had convinced Lane of the need to procure food from elsewhere. Pemisipan encouraged the governor and his men to journey up the Albemarle Sound for trade and additional reasons as well. The weroance informed Lane that the native copper source was to the west. Furthermore, he told the colony leader that the Chawanoacs, Ossomocomuck's most powerful tribe, were planning to annihilate the English. Pemisipan simultaneously had a message delivered to the Chawanoacs. In it, he asserted that the colonists intended to assault the Chawanoac's largest village. Pemisipan lured Lane and his men into the hostile territory of his strongest native neighbors with the prospects of obtaining food, preempting an impending attack, and controlling the native copper trade. Although the English brought copper to Ossomocomuck to trade, they also hoped that the region would help them in various mineralogical pursuits and were eager to locate the nearest Algonquian copper source (Hudgins 2004). The Roanoac leader hoped that his scheme would eliminate the English while simultaneously weakening the rival Chawanoacs in the process.

Never one to wait for an attack, Lane took the bait. He and his men burst into the Chawanoac center and immediately seized and placed Chief Menatonon, who had lost the use of his legs years earlier, in shackles (Quinn 1955:259). The Chawanoac weroance ignored this affront. Instead of the abduction leading to further hostility, Menatonon offered gifts to Lane. He presented the governor with pearls and also offered guides to help him investigate adjacent territories (Quinn 1955:260, 261, 270). These presents established friendly relations between the English and Chawanoacs. Even when the colonists failed to reciprocate for these gifts—an economic transgression that in other instances had provoked alienation and abandonment—the alliance stayed strong. Pemisipan's plan, instead of weakening two formidable Roanoac adversaries, generated an alliance.

Attempting to locate the area's indigenous copper source, Lane freed Menatonon and used the chief's son Skiko as a guide. The English had little food with them and intended to trade copper to the Moratucs and Mangoaks for maize on their trip westward. Pemisipan subverted these plans by sending word to the indigenous population along the Roanoke River that Lane's party had come to destroy them. Lane explained the weroance's exploits, writing that, "[Pemisipan] sent worde to the Mangoaks of [my] intention to . . . kill them (as he sayd) both they and the Moratiks . . . abandoned their Townes along the Riuer, and retyred themselues with their Crenpoes [women], and their corne within the mayne [mainland]" (Quinn 1955:270). The Roanoac chief had successfully convinced the other tribes to avoid the visiting colonists.

The English continued up the Roanoke River and heard a group of nearby natives singing. Just as one of the native guides explained that Ossomocomuck serenades of this type frequently preceded violence, the Mangoaks launched an attack but failed to injure any of the crew. The assault convinced Lane to forsake the quest for nourishment, new exchange partners, and the native copper source. The English reversed course and headed back to their settlement. Since Lane could find no one with whom to exchange for food, he and his men were forced to eat the two dogs he had brought along on the trip to foil Pemisipan's nearly successful plan of starving them. The English team survived on a "pottage of sassafras leaues" and "dog porredge" (Quinn 1955:272). The governor and his men then sailed down the Roanoke River and entered the Albemarle Sound, where they encountered native fishing traps near the Weapemeoc village of Chipanum. The Weapemeocs, following Pemisipan's warnings, had also deserted their towns along the river. As a result, there were no natives to prevent the English from helping themselves to the fish that had been caught in the Weapemeoc weirs.

Lane's return stunned the Roanoacs, especially Pemisipan who had prematurely boasted of successfully eliminating the colony leader. Ensenore, an influential Roanoac elder, believed that the governor and his men were ghosts and had come back from the dead. He told Lane that, "being dead men [the English] were able to doe them [the natives] more hurt" (Quinn 1955:278). In general, Algonquians across North America held individuals who apparently possessed the power to rejuvenate or resuscitate in great esteem. Jamestown colonist William Strachey asserted that the Powhatans saw these abilities as "divine" and the result of "an infusion of godliness" (Strachey 1953:60–61). Anthropologist A. Irving Hallowell noted a similar trend among the Algonquian-speaking Ojibwas, a group of native tribes living in Michigan, Wisconsin, Minnesota, and North Dakota. He wrote that people with "the [alleged] power to cure" themselves or others "occupy a special position . . . [and] outrank other men in power" (Hallowell 1976:432–433). Lane's return, a seeming supernatural revival, greatly impressed Ensenore as did his abduction of the powerful rival weroance and his son Skiko. This native elder, believed by Lane to be Pemisipan's father, consequently declared that the Roanoac chief should cease hostile actions toward the English. Ensenore absolved the colonists of their previous transgressions and mandated friendly relations.

Did the Algonquians really believe that Lane had returned from the dead, or was this another instance of Europeans thinking that the native population saw them as gods? The surrounding details of the contemporary historical sources emphasized the change in Algonquian behavior following Lane's return and his purported mystical power of self-regeneration. Although the concern regarding European constructions of their own perceived deification is important to note, the context of these events pinpoints a marked change in native perception (Obeyesekere 1992:134). This transformation stemmed from an immediate surge in Lane's status in Algonquian eyes that corresponded with a specific historical sequence and a perceived supernatural talent. The natives did not necessarily view Lane as their god or as any specific god that corresponded with their cultural belief system. But they did attribute to him a change in ability and, thus, status.

## Period IV: First Colony—the Last Months of Settlement (April–June 1586)

Ensenore not only convinced Pemisipan to rescind his anti-English policies, he also induced the Roanoac weroance to revert to sustaining the colonists. Ensenore insisted that Pemisipan "set vp [fishing] weares," "sow a good quantitie of ground," and provide "dayly . . . supply of victuall [food]" for the settlers (Quinn 1955:279–280). Once again, the English failed to compensate the natives for these goods and services. In violating the Algonquian gift economy by refusing to reciprocate and denying the alliance, the settlers symbolically pushed the natives away. Past events in the Chesapeake had suggested that the expected punishment for this transgression was separation. Since gift recipients were allotted a certain amount of time to compensate their benefactors, the abandonment was not immediate. At Ajacan, the Algonquians waited a few weeks. At Roanoke, Pemisipan and his followers deserted the colonists less than 17 days after the English transgression.

Lane still detained Skiko. Menatonon made an offering—"a pearl for a present, or . . . the ransome of his sonne"—that Lane refused (Quinn 1955:279–280). The Chawanoac chief simply ignored the slight as he had with previous European economic violations. In fact, Menatonon's emissary then offered the English an additional gift. Menatonon, who indirectly commanded the Weapemeocs and their weroance Okisko as well as the Chawanoacs, sent 24 of Okisko's warriors along with his courier to Lane. These natives declared that both the Chawanoacs and the Weapemeocs now served England. Lane described their proclamation, reporting that, "[Menatonon] commaunded Okisko king of Weopomoik to yelde himselfe seruant, and homager, to the great Weroanza of England [Queen Elizabeth I], . . . the sayd Okisko . . . sent foure and twentie of his principallest men to Roanoak . . . , to signifie that they were readie to perfourme the same . . . [Menatonon] had sent those men to let [Lane] knowe, that from that time forwards hee [Menatonon] and his successours were to acknowledge her Maiestie [as] their onely Soueraigne [sovereign]" (Quinn 1955:279).

This gift from Menatonon further solidified the Chawanoac/English bond in spite of the governor's previous refusals. More importantly for the natives, through the offering Menatonon had completely surrounded Pemisipan's people with English allies and Roanoac adversaries (Figure 4.1). To the west and southwest were the Secotans, established enemies of the Roanoacs who had nearly killed Pemisipan (Wingina) years earlier. And to the southeast were the Croatoans, a tribe of Algonquians who had maintained a continual alliance with the colonists. To the north and northwest were the Weapemeocs and Chawanoacs, the newest subjects of the English monarch. To the west and southwest were the Croatoans, a tribe of Algonquians who had maintained a continual alliance with the colonists. Menatonon, who faced initial English hostility solely because of Pemisipan's schemes, bolstered the presence of the First Colony in Roanoac territory by establishing an accord among the settlers, Chawanoacs,

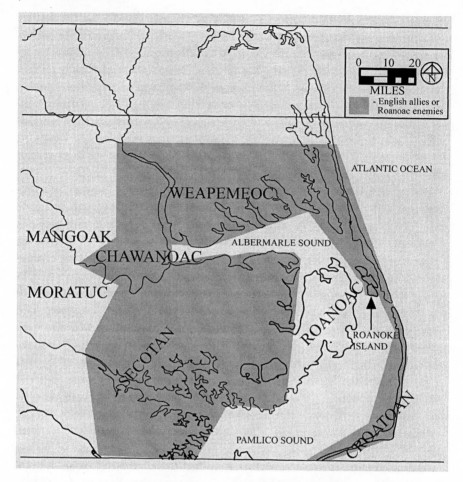

Figure 4.1. Ossomocomuck balance of power after Chawanoac gift

and Weapemeocs. The Chawanoac chief skillfully manipulated the Ossomocomuck political alliances so that the Roanoacs either would have to coexist
with the burdensome English colony and their impulsive leader or attack a
group of settlers who were suddenly supported by numerous powerful indigenous neighbors.

When Ensenore died on April 20, 1586, Pemisipan immediately ended his
support and tolerance of the European settlement. Lane described Ensenore as
"the only frend . . . [the English] had amongst" the Roanoacs and likened him
to Granganimeo (Quinn 1955:275). Ensenore and Granganimeo were both in-

fluential Algonquian liaisons who bonded with the colonists through repeated gift exchange. Ensenore's passing, like Granganimeo's, resulted in the loss of the highest ranking English ally among the Roanoacs. The death of an elite exchange partner, combined with settler failures to reciprocate Roanoac gifts, again provoked indigenous hostility.

Having obtained European copper through previous exchanges with the English, Pemisipan attempted to use this prestigious good to hire fellow Ossomocomuck natives to attack the First Colony. Pemisipan could afford this investment. In addition to his substantial current holdings, the Roanoac weroance anticipated being able to replenish his copper supplies once he annihilated the English settlement and absorbed their possessions. Pemisipan's plan to eliminate Lane and his followers relied on three strategies. First, the Roanoacs refused to exchange any food with the English. The governor noted that the natives "agreed . . . that they should not for any copper, sell vs any victuals whatsoeuer" (Quinn 1955:282). In addition, most of the Algonquians abandoned their villages at Roanoke Island and moved to Dasemunkepeuc, a nearby Roanoac settlement on the mainland across the Croatoan Sound, thus isolating the English. Second, the natives destroyed one of the few English food sources, the settlers' fishing weirs. Third, the Roanoacs planned a direct assault on the First Colony. Lane wrote that the goal of this attack was to "knock out my braynes" (Quinn 1955:282).

Maintaining an alliance with the Chawanoacs provided Lane with privileged information regarding the intent and identity of natives who were assembling at Dasemunkepeuc during May of 1586. Skiko still resided at Fort Ralegh, and he gladly spied on the Roanoacs for the English. The Chawanoac prince informed Lane that hundreds of natives, including Weapemeocs, Mangoaks, Chesepians, and Secotans, lured with promises of copper were meeting to coordinate an attack on the settlers led by Pemisipan. When analyzed as a whole, four seemingly anomalous individual Chawanoac acts revealed Menatonon's genius and attention to reciprocal vengeance—(1) enduring an initial English attack without fighting back, (2) not punishing the colonists for failing to reciprocate and refusing an offer, (3) giving themselves and the Weapemeocs to the settlers, and (4) informing Lane of the impending multitribal assault. The Chawanoac chief employed Pemisipan's own tactics against him, using the colonists as a tool to fight the Roanoacs. In order to avenge Pemisipan's ploy of baiting the English to attack the Chawanoacs in March of 1586, Menatonon ignored the settlers' socioeconomic affronts, manipulated Ossomocomuck intertribal relations, and had his son reveal the coming aggression to the colonists. The Chawanoac weroance had already witnessed firsthand Lane's propensity to attack groups rumored to be planning an assault on the English. The Chawanoacs, following Algonquian norms, retaliated in kind for the Roanoac-inspired English assault. They provoked an English attack on the Roanoacs.

When Lane heard of the looming indigenous attack, he immediately devised a set of tactics to stall and preempt the native strike. The governor falsely declared that his men had spotted English supply ships nearing the Carolinas. He duplicitously asked Pemisipan and his followers to secure food for a trip to meet the arriving reinforcements. Lane then ordered an attack on the few Roanoacs still at Roanoke Island. In an attempt to prevent the natives from warning others of English aggression, the governor sent a few of his men to collect the Algonquian canoes. These colonists encountered two Roanoacs and decapitated them. Other natives joined the fray, and the English opened fire. Lane reported that, "three or foure of [the Roanoacs] at first were slayne with our shot, the rest fled into ye woods" (Quinn 1955:285).

Meanwhile, natives from all over the Carolinas met at Dasemunkepeuc with Pemisipan to discuss their impending wholesale attack on the First Colony. Lane and his men secretly ventured to the mainland to confront the Roanoac weroance and his supporters. The English burst into Dasemunkepeuc and on Lane's command his soldiers opened fire. The governor thought that his men had killed the Roanoac chief who lay on the ground "shot thorow," but Pemisipan had a final surprise in store for the colonists (Quinn 1955:287). Lane explained that the Roanoac leader "suddenly . . . started vp, and ran away as though he had not bene touched" (Quinn 1955:287). A few of the colonists chased after Pemisipan and eventually beheaded him.

With little food, few trade options, and dreading retribution for the murder of the Roanoac weroance, the colonists longed for the overdue English supply ships. Fresh from successfully attacking various Spanish settlements in the Americas, English buccaneer Francis Drake arrived at Roanoke Island a few days after Lane's assault on the natives. The settlers celebrated Drake's arrival, although he did not visit with the intent of replenishing the colony. Drake made two offers to Lane. The governor could take two of his ships and explore the Chesapeake, or he and the settlers could return with Drake to England. Lane realized that the colonists had worn out their welcome in the Carolinas but wanted to accomplish more before traveling home. As a result, he initially opted to explore the Chesapeake. Just as the settlers began to load their supplies and board the vessels a four-day storm pounded the Outer Banks. It destroyed much of the English fleet off of Roanoke Island. Drake no longer had ships to spare for a possible Chesapeake venture. Seeing the ravaged vessels, Lane amended his previous decision and requested that Drake take the colonists back to England. Visions of native revenge and torrential downpour sped their departure on June 18, 1586. In their haste, Lane and his men abandoned three colonists, who had likely gone to Chawanoac to return Skiko to his father (Quinn 1955:307).

In the two months between the First Colony's departure from the Carolinas and Grenville's arrival at Roanoke Island with reinforcements, the indigenous population likely hanged two individuals, one English and one native. Grenville discovered the suspended corpses in August of 1586. Archaeologist Ivor Noël Hume concluded that by the time Grenville came to the abandoned settlement the bodies had only recently been hanged. He deduced that, "the weight of the decaying cadavers would have separated them from their heads in a few summer weeks" (Noël Hume 1994:55). The English body, likely belonging to one of the three colonists that Lane had abandoned, must have been hung after Lane's crew had left the Americas.

## Period V: Second Colony (August 1586)

Upon their arrival in the Carolinas, Grenville and his crew seized three natives in order to learn the whereabouts of the First Colony, not knowing they had since departed abruptly with Drake. Pedro Diaz related the testimony of one of the captives, who explained that, "Francisco Draque [Drake] had brought away the [English] people who had been on [Roanoke] island" (Quinn 1955:790). Even though Raleigh had given Grenville strict orders to leave 150 men at Roanoke, the general placed only 15 to 18 soldiers at the deserted village and then embarked on a highly profitable four-month privateering venture (Quinn 1955:789).

As soon as Grenville departed, 30 natives from the villages of Aquascococke, Dasemunkepeuc, and Secotan promptly attacked these Second Colonists. The Algonquians, "through their nimbleness" and greater numbers, quickly overwhelmed the settlers (Quinn 1955:528). Nine of the English managed to escape the island by boat and regrouped with four of their comrades who had been searching for oysters. These 13 colonists then made their way to "a little Island on the right hand of [the] entrance into the harbour of Hatorask," never to be seen again by Europeans (Quinn 1955:528). The Second Colony faced indigenous hostility inspired by the actions of the First Colony. Grenville's burning of Aquascococke in July of 1585 and Lane's assault on Dasemunkepeuc in June of 1586 united the Roanoacs and Secotans in their hatred of the English. These former native adversaries forced future Carolina colonists to suffer for the deeds of their English predecessors.

*Period VI: Third Colony (1587–90)*

Although Raleigh's enthusiasm regarding the Roanoke ventures had waned by 1587, artist John White now championed the establishment of an English settlement in the North American Middle Atlantic. White led a group of 110 individuals, including English men, women, and children, and Carolina Algonquians Manteo and Towaye to the Americas. Due to the recent hostilities with Ossomocomuck natives, White and his crew intended to settle the Chesapeake, not Roanoke Island. They first wanted to check on the men Grenville had left at the fort a year earlier but then planned on venturing northward. Three ships set sail for the Outer Banks from England on May 8, 1587. Almost immediately, White and Simao Fernandes, the ship's pilot, struggled for control of the venture (Quinn 1955:503). Fernandes refused to take the settlers to the Chesapeake. White initially disputed the decision but ultimately consented. As a result, for the third consecutive time, the English tried to establish a permanent colony at Roanoke Island. Why did White agree to another attempted colony in the Carolinas? Quinn suggested three possible reasons. First, White might have feared that a confrontation with the pilot would endanger the women and children on board. Second, the colony leader was generally characterized as a timid man. Third, perhaps White intended to settle there all along (Quinn 1984:279).

Once in the Outer Banks, White immediately discovered the lifeless remains of one of Grenville's reinforcements. Soon afterward, the Third Colony faced indigenous hostility from the Roanoac/Secotan alliance. A mere six days after their arrival in the Carolinas, a settler named George Howe made the mistake of wandering off in search of crabs. The Algonquians immediately set upon him, giving "him sixteene wounds with their arrowes: and . . . beat[ing] his head in peeces" (Quinn 1955:525–526). White realized the need for native allies and dispatched some of his men with Manteo to visit the Croatoans, a tribe who had always supported the settlers. The Third Colony leader listed the three tasks he gave the group: "[1] vnderstande some newes of our fifteene men [the Second Colony], . . . [2] learne the disposition of the [indigenous] people of the Countrey towards vs, and [3] renew our olde friendshippe with [the Croatoans]" (Quinn 1955:526).

Once the team of settlers and Croatoans met and Manteo assured his native kin of the colonists' peaceful intentions, these natives held a feast for the English. When recounting events of the past few years to White and his men during the celebratory meal, the Croatoans informed the settlers that Lane had inadvertently killed some of their people in his assault on the Roanoacs in June of 1586. Manteo's people maintained that they told the English of these assaults not to anger or humiliate them but to demonstrate why they needed some sort of marker or badge that would allow the colonists to distinguish them, the Croatoans, from other Algonquians. Later events suggested that these natives never received any sort of markers from the colonists. The Croatoans described the Roanoac/Secotan attack on the Second Colony and explained that these Algonquians were also responsible for the slaughter of Howe. After hearing this information, White requested that Manteo's kin make a peace offering to other Ossomocomuck natives on the behalf of the English. He asked the Croatoans to propose friendship to the people of "Secota, Aquascogoc, & Pomiock," assuring them that the colonists "would willingly receaue them againe and that all vnfriendly dealings of the past on both parties, should be vtterly forgotten" (Quinn 1955:527). The Croatoans accepted the mission and attempted to secure peace for the settlers. White gave the Roanoacs and Secotans a week to respond to his offer.

Seven days passed without any reply. Instead of sending another plea for amity or waiting longer, White made immediate plans to avenge the loss of the Second Colony and the murder of Howe. Earlier the Croatoans had informed the English that the Roanoacs had regrouped after the 1586 decapitation of Pemisipan under new joint Roanoac/Secotan leadership at Dasemunkepeuc. White sent Captain Stafford and 24 men to attack the village on the evening of August 8, 1587. The soldiers hid in the woods along the edge of Dasemunkepeuc and started their assault moments before the sun rose the next morning. They attacked and quickly vanquished their foes. English glory turned to shame when the soldiers realized they had again mistakenly assaulted the Croatoans. The Roanoacs and Secotans, fearing English retribution, had abandoned Dasemunkepeuc after killing Howe.

A few days later, the English rewarded Croatoan prince Manteo for his loyal service over the course of the previous weeks (Quinn 1955:527). They made him a vassal of their queen and deemed him Lord of Roanoke and Dasemunkepeuc. This English offering of title and authority continued the exclusive gift exchange—except for friendly fire—between the Croatoans and the settlers.

The transatlantic voyage had severely depleted the colonists' supplies. The settlers doubted their chances of surviving the coming winter. They concluded that the only way to guarantee prompt arrival of additional provisions was to send White back to England. Although his granddaughter Virginia Dare, the first Anglo-American, had been born only a few days earlier at Roanoke Island, a reluctant John White agreed to the plan (Quinn 1955:505). As he prepared to leave the Outer Banks, the colonists discussed relocating their settlement to the Chesapeake. White instructed them to carve the name of their intended destination on a tree if they moved. He also told the settlers to inscribe a Maltese cross if they faced mortal danger. White left the 114 colonists at Roanoke Island in November of 1587.

The years from 1587 to 1589 were extraordinarily frustrating for John White (Quinn 1955:505). The Spanish/English conflict escalated; war was declared on October 9, 1587. Due to the heightened hostilities, Queen Elizabeth prohibited ships from departing England for the Americas (Quinn 1955:300). White attempted a trip to the Carolinas in 1588, but French pirates attacked, stripped his ship, and forced its return. Even though the English navy defeated the Spanish Armada on July 31, 1588, White continued to experience difficulties in procuring transportation to Roanoke Island. In May of 1590, White joined the *Hopewell* and her captain, Abraham Cocke, on a transatlantic journey. Two months later, the *Moonlight*, led by John Watts, joined Cocke's contingency. The ships reached the Carolinas in August. Cocke sent two pinnaces to investigate a possible smoke signal and lost a ship and seven men in the process. After the mishap, many of Cocke's crew insisted on leaving the area, yet Cocke refused to quit the Americas without first visiting Roanoke Island.

He sent White and some of his crew ashore to search for the colonists. Upon approaching the remains of the abandoned fort, they saw the letters "CRO" incised into a tree, the word "CROATOAN" scraped on a nearby post, and no sign of a Maltese cross (Quinn 1955:327). Having witnessed the agreed-upon markers of movement, White concluded that the colonists had gone to stay with Manteo at one of the nearby Croatoan settlements on the islands in the Outer Banks. Upon seeing his former Roanoke settlement in shambles and many of his own goods torn to pieces, White concluded that the Roanoacs and Secotans were the perpetrators of this raid as well. He declared that, "This could bee no other but the deede of the Sauages our [Roanoac and Secotan] enemies at Dasamongwepeuk, who had watched the departure of our men to Croatoan; and asoone as they were departed, digged vp euery place where they suspected any thing to be buried" (Quinn 1955:327).

A storm then struck, preventing White from thoroughly searching the islands and causing extensive damage to Cocke's vessels. Left with few working cables and anchors, Cocke and his crew, including a despondent John White, decided to return to England. Before leaving, they fired their guns in hopes of attracting the attention of any nearby settlers who might hear them and respond with a signal of their own. These blasts went unanswered and the location of the "Lost Colonists" remained a mystery. Raleigh sent two ships to search for the settlers in 1603, but they failed to find White's former colleagues as well. Chief Powhatan would later boast in 1606 that he had murdered the

Table 4.1. Exchange lists for the different Ossomocomuck tribes

English/Secotan interaction

| Exchange number | Exchange type | Exchange system violation | Consequences |
|---|---|---|---|
| 48 | Other | 1. Theft; violates commodity economy and requires compensation | 1. English demand return of stolen good |
| 49 | Gift | | |
| 50 | Other | 2. Broken promise; violates commodity economy and requires retribution | 2. English burn Aquascococke |
| 51, 57, 78, 85, 89, 100 | Other/ Violence | | |

English/Chawanoac interaction

| Exchange number | Exchange type | Exchange system violation | Consequences |
|---|---|---|---|
| 61 | Other/ Violence | | |
| 62–64 | Gift | 1. Failure to reciprocate; violates gift economy, and is a refusal of alliance | 1. No response |
| 66 | Commodity/ Gift | | |
| 72 | Other | 2. Failure to accept; violates gift economy and socially diminishes partner | 2. No response |
| 74 | Gift | | |

English/Croatoan interaction

| Exchange number | Exchange type | Exchange system violation | Consequences |
|---|---|---|---|
| 47 | Gift | | |
| 85 | Other/ Violence | 1. Hostility toward gift-exchange partner; violates gift economy and disrupts alliance | 1. No response |
| 91 | Gift | | |

*Continues on the next page*

Table 4.1 *Continued*

| Exchange number | Exchange type | Exchange system violation | Consequences |
|---|---|---|---|
| 92 | Other | | |
| 93–96 | Gift | | |
| 97 | Other/ Violence | 2. Hostility toward gift-exchange partner; violates gift economy and disrupts alliance | 2. No response |
| 99 | Gift | | |

English/Weapemeoc interaction

| Exchange number | Exchange type |
|---|---|
| 68 | Other/Violence |
| 70 | Other |
| 85 | Other/Violence |

English/Mangoak interaction

| Exchange number | Exchange type |
|---|---|
| 68 | Other/Violence |
| 69 | Other/Violence |
| 78, 85 | Other/Violence |

English/Chesepian interaction

| Exchange number | Exchange type |
|---|---|
| 68 | Other/Violence |

English/ Moratuc interaction

| Exchange number | Exchange type |
|---|---|
| 78, 85 | Other/Violence |

Lost Colonists when they ventured into the Chesapeake on a trading mission (Strachey 1953:91).

## Roanoke Exchange Patterns

The colonists engaged eight different Ossomocomuck tribes—Roanoacs, Secotans, Chawanoacs, Croatoans, Weapemeocs, Mangoaks, Chesepians, and Moratucs —and maintained strikingly different relations with each group (Table 4.1). Relations with some tribes, like the Croatoans, were entirely amicable even though the natives were repeatedly victimized by English friendly fire casualties. Conversely, the Mangoaks, Chesepians, and Moratucs only met the settlers with hostilities. Other tribes maintained ambiguous ties to the English, always with an eye on the fluctuating Carolina political tide. The Weapemeocs acknowledged the rule of the English monarch when it served them to be on the side of the mighty Chawanoacs one week and prepared to "knock out [Lane's] braynes" with the Roanoacs, Secotans, Mangoaks, and Chesepians the next (Quinn 1955:282).

After Grenville burned the Secotan village of Aquascococke, the Secotans determined the English to be their enemies. However, these Algonquians were unable to attack the colonists because their settlement was well within Roanoac territory, and the Secotans and Roanoacs were enemies at the time. In order to avenge Grenville's hostilities, the Secotans would have had to cross into either Roanoac or Croatoan territory; both were home to formidable English allies. As soon as the settlers had antagonized the Roanoacs, however, the Secotans made amends with their indigenous neighbors to the east and repeatedly assaulted the English.

English/Roanoac relations flourished momentarily during 1584, prior to colonization. However, they soured after European diseases devastated indigenous villages and in turn their alliances. The Roanoacs attempted to remove the English by baiting them into attacking the Chawanoacs. The move backfired when the Chawanoacs endured this slight and others. The Chawanoacs, employing reciprocal deceit and following the dynamics of gift exchange, avenged the Roanoac scheme by successfully luring the English into annihilating the Roanoacs. The overall Ossomocomuck balance of power serves to explain the logic of otherwise perplexing and erratic Algonquian responses to English transgressions. Potential gains in political power often superseded retaliation for socioeconomic affronts.

# 5
# *Jamestown*

Undeterred by three failed colonies in the Carolinas, England attempted another Middle Atlantic settlement in the early 1600s. This Jamestown colony would succeed in becoming the first permanent English settlement in the Americas. Much like the ill-fated European colonies at Ajacan and Roanoke, socioeconomic clashes contributed to intercultural hostilities at early Jamestown. The English faced seven sets of Powhatan attacks during their initial five years in the Chesapeake. Although the first was unprovoked, economic violations by the colonists likely played a role in all but one of the others. In fact, excluding interaction with the Nansamund tribe, all of the Powhatan hostilities with the English followed specific European exchange transgressions.

## The History

Fluctuating English/Powhatan relations divided the first five years of European settlement at Jamestown into the following 11 periods of alternating hostility and alliance:

(1) Initial ambiguity; April–June, 1607,
(2) Peace; June–October, 1607,
(3) First inundation and the search for untapped food sources; October–December, 1607,
(4) Abduction; December, 1607,
(5) Adoption, peace, and second inundation; January–March, 1608,
(6) Deteriorating relations; March–June, 1608,
(7) Chesapeake exploration; June–August, 1608,
(8) Third inundation; September, 1608–January, 1609,

(9) Assassination attempts; January–August, 1609,

(10) Resuscitation; August–September, 1609, and

(11) Smith's departure and war; October, 1609–1611.

Unlike the case studies of Ajacan and Roanoke that dealt with dozens of exchanges, contemporary historical records of Jamestown detailed hundreds of transactions between colonists and the indigenous population during the first five years of this English settlement. As a result, this chapter summarizes the exchange patterns by period instead of visiting each of them individually.

*Period I: Initial Ambiguity; April–June 1607*

Over 100 colonists set sail from the London area for the Chesapeake on the evening of December 19, 1606, aboard three English ships, the *Susan Constant*, the *Godspeed*, and the *Discovery*. Led by Captain Christopher Newport, an experienced commander who had already spent time in the West Indies, the fleet endured many transatlantic storms during the four-month journey. After entering the Chesapeake Bay at Cape Henry, the English made their first landfall on the evening of April 26, 1607. Captain Newport led 30 men ashore, whom "certaine Indians" promptly assaulted (Smith et al. 1986, 1:27). None of the primary sources specified the tribe that had led the attack. However, Newport avenged the violence a year later on natives he held responsible—the Nansamunds. The Nansamunds were the only Powhatan tribe to engage the English in repeated hostilities not immediately preceded by exchange violations. It is also worth noting that the Nansamunds lived at the south edge of the Powhatan chiefdom in an area that bordered the Carolina's Ossomocomuck territory. The Nansamunds neighbored the Chesepians, a Powhatan tribe that had participated in assaults against the Roanoke colonies in the 1580s. Therefore, this initial attack on the Jamestown settlers might have also been a continuation of unresolved Roanoke hostilities.

During the week following the colonists' arrival in the Chesapeake Bay, English interaction with the local indigenous population improved. Kecoughtans welcomed and feasted the colonists. Newport requited them for the offerings, presenting the natives with beads. Within a few days, the settlers journeyed into Paspahegh territory, the future site of James Fort. There the Algonquians elaborately entertained the colonists. The settlers did not reward the Paspaheghs for their hospitality. This omission of reciprocity was the first of four consecutive English failures to compensate the Paspaheghs for their offerings. These occurred in a matter of a few weeks, and each of these violations of Algonquian gift-exchange norms alienated the natives. The first in this series of offenses took place between the colonists and Chief Pemiscuminah, the leader of nearby Quiyoughcohannock. Chief Pemiscuminah sent a message to the colonists, inviting them to visit. Newport accepted the offer and presented trifles to the natives who delivered the summons. The messenger then led the English to his village. The colonists requited the messenger for his guidance but failed to compensate Pemiscuminah for "entertain[ing them] in good humanitie" (Barbour 1969 I:137). In failing to reciprocate to the Quiyoughcohannock weroance, the English again transgressed indigenous socioeconomic standards.

The next offense took place one week later when two Paspahegh messengers visited the settlers and announced that their weroance, Chief Wowinchopunk, was coming to present the colonists with a large deer. The Algonquian leader kept his promise and also offered the English "as much land as [they] would desire to take" (Barbour 1969, 1:139). The settlers did not compensate the Paspaheghs for these offerings, again symbolically denying them. During the visit, one of the natives stole a hatchet. A colonist snatched it back from the Algonquian culprit, striking him in the process. Other natives rushed to the defense of their comrade. The confrontation escalated; the English drew their weapons. On the verge of bloodshed from unrequited gifts, an infuriated Wowinchopunk stormed out of the English camp with his men.

The Paspahegh theft was an attempt at forcing reciprocity from the English, an action merited according to the rules of the indigenous gift economy. The event paralleled the Aquascocockian silver cup incident in the Carolinas 22 years earlier. Just as Secotan natives stole an item from the English after the colonists failed to reciprocate, the Paspaheghs attempted to secure material compensation from recently obliged colonists by taking a hatchet. Both Algonquian responses to the gift-exchange violation, however, transgressed the commodity economy. Whereas Grenville and his men burned Aquascococke as punishment, a Jamestown colonist grabbed the hatchet back from the Paspahegh native and assaulted him in the process. Tensions between the Paspaheghs and settlers appeared to ease on May 20, 1607, when Wowinchopunk sent another gift of deer to the English. Although the colonists anticipated hostilities, the natives merely delivered the gift of food and left. Yet again, the English did not reciprocate.

The next day, Newport, Smith, and 20 other settlers set off in a shallop on an exploratory mission up the James River. They promptly encountered the Weanocks who entertained and feasted them (Smith et al. 1986, 1:29, 82). Newport rewarded the natives, "kindely requit[ing] their least favours with Bels, Pinnes, Needles, [and] beades" (Smith et al. 1986, 1:29). Gifts between the settlers and the Weanocks established friendly relations and led to widespread trading. The Weanocks and Paspaheghs were currently adversaries. Smith noted that the Weanocks "Demonstrated . . . [the] hurtes [injuries]" that they had suffered at the hands of Wowinchopunk and his followers (Smith et al. 1986, 1:82). Thus, the English, who in the past weeks had repeatedly snubbed the Paspaheghs, engaged current Paspahegh adversaries who also participated in the competitive Powhatan tribute system. Although the earlier economic transgressions by the colonists had merely alienated the Paspaheghs and denied their alliance, these exchanges with social rivals diminished and humiliated Wowinchopunk's people. The English offered prestigious goods to the Weanocks that they had denied the Paspaheghs. Thirty-seven years earlier at Ajacan, a parallel sequence of unintended slights contributed to lethal indigenous aggression. The English had inadvertently put themselves in a similar situation, jeopardizing their relationship with neighboring Algonquians through socioeconomic transgressions.

Over the next few days, Newport and his crew encountered natives from a variety of Powhatan villages, including Arrohattoc, Tanx Powhatan, Kind Woman's Care, Queen Appamattuck's Bower, and an unspecified Pamunkey town. The English and indigenous population at each of these native settlements regaled each other and solidified peaceful relations. While Newport and his men were exchanging gifts with the Pamunkeys on May 25, 1607, the Paspaheghs led a multitribal attack against James Fort. Wowinchopunk and as many as 400 other Algonquians furiously assaulted the English settlement, killing two and injuring at least 17 colonists (Barbour 1969, 1:95). Newport and his men returned to their battered Jamestown compound and subsequently faced five more Algonquian attacks from the same native adversaries.

Two natives whom Newport recognized as allies from his recent exploration of the surrounding area arrived at James Fort on June 14, 1607, with information for the English. The Algonquians listed the indigenous allies and enemies of the settlers. They specified that the Pamunkeys, Arrohattocs, Youghtanunds, and Mattapanients supported the colonists. On the contrary, the Paspaheghs, Quiyoughcohannocks, Appamattucks, and Kiskiacks resented the Europeans. The Powhatan tribes that played the most significant role in the assault on the colonists, the Paspaheghs and the Quiyoughcohannocks, were largely the same groups that the settlers failed to compensate for indigenous gifts.

English economic transgressions had alienated, diminished, and, thus, provoked Paspahegh and Quiyoughcohannock attacks. Newport and his crew did not requite four separate Paspahegh offerings. Wowinchopunk and his followers initially waited for return items from the settlers, but none came. The Paspaheghs then attempted to take compensation from the colonists, which nearly resulted in bloodshed. A final English failure to reciprocate completed the literal and symbolic alienation of the Paspaheghs. When the colonists then requited other tribes within the same competitive tribute system as the Paspaheghs—especially the Weanocks who were Paspahegh adversaries—they humiliated Wowinchopunk and his followers. The settlers diminished the Quiyoughco-hannocks in the same manner. Although Newport adequately rewarded the messenger for delivering Pemiscuminah's invitation, he never compensated the weroance for the feast. Thus, the surrounding Chesapeake tribes consisted of two groups with respect to the attack on the English; those that partook in the siege after being economically wronged by the colonists and those that had bonded with the colonists through reciprocal gift exchange.

The colonists' decisions to exchange with certain Algonquian tribes reflected a distinct geographic pattern. The farther they ventured from the fort, the more magnanimous they became. The settlers repeatedly regaled these more distant indigenous groups. Conversely, Algonquian tribes close to Jamestown, the Paspaheghs and Quiyoughcohannocks, received neither initial gifts nor recip-rocal offerings. The Kiskiacks lived near James Fort and likely witnessed this pattern. They too joined in the Algonquian assault on the colonists.

Virginia Company leaders in London would later enact policy that reflected this pattern. In 1609 they informed Jamestown's Council that, "If you make friendship with any of these [native] nations as you must doe, choose to doe it with those that are farthest from you and enemies unto those amonge whom you dwell, for you shall have the least occasion to have differences with them and by that means a suerer league of amity" (Potter 1989:158). London officials, anticipating that conflict was inevitable between the colonists and nearby na-tives, advised the settlers to form an alliance with distant tribes that would be less likely to antagonize or be antagonized by the English. The colonists would repeat these tactics on a larger scale in 1609 when they chose to embrace native groups from outside of the Powhatan chiefdom at the expense of good rela-tions with Chief Powhatan (Potter 1989:158).

*Period II: Peace; June–October, 1607*

With the passing of spring came an end to hostilities from native tribes adja-cent to the English settlement. Reciprocal gifts between these natives and set-tlers established an alliance and prevented the colonists from starving during their initial summer at Jamestown. On June 25, 1607, an Algonquian represent-ing Chief Powhatan offered peace to the colonists and ensured that all of his followers, even the Paspaheghs, would be friendly. Newport returned to En-gland confident in the prospects of the Virginia Company's new settlement.

From July to September 1607, the food that the natives brought to James Fort saved the colony. The historical records offered general accounts of English/ Powhatan trade during this time, yet even with the native sustenance, the disease-ridden settlers struggled to survive the Virginia summer (Smith et al. 1986, 1:35, 218; Barbour 1969, 1:145). Smith reported that, "God (being angrie with us) plagued us with such famin and sicknes, that the living were scarce able to bury the dead" (Smith et al. 1986, 1:33). In fact, he noted that most colonists "were sicke almost to death, untill they were seasoned to the country" (Smith et al. 1986, 2:170). Once settlers endured a Virginia summer, Smith observed that they developed a tolerance for the Middle Atlantic and its ailments.

*Period III: First Inundation and the Search for Untapped Food Sources; October–December, 1607*

The English had flooded native society with European trade goods during the late summer and early fall of 1607. This was soon followed by a distinct decline in trade. With the colony's sizable demands on the native food surplus, Smith observed that, "the Salvages superfluity [began] to decrease" (Smith et al. 1986, 1:211). The Cape Merchant, while venturing downriver on an official trade mission in search of provisions at Kecoughtan, noted that the natives scorned him. He reported that these Algonquians "in derision offer[ed] him" scant amounts of food—"a handfull of Corne, a peece of bread"—in exchange for European goods that in the past had garnered entire hogsheads of corn (Smith et al. 1986, 2:144).

By the second week in November, Smith found trade with nearby natives nearly impossible. He failed in an attempt to trade with the Quiyoughcohannocks, noting that the natives had food to spare but chose not to exchange with the English (Smith et al. 1986, 1:37, 39). On another occasion, Smith struggled to acquire 10 bushels of corn from the Paspaheghs. This trade was full of deception, however, as Smith revealed that the "churlish and trecherous" natives "dogged" the settlers and tried to attack them during the trade (Smith et al. 1986, 1:39). Days later other settlers attempted trade with the Paspaheghs but were entirely unsuccessful.

Smith attributed these refusals to exchange to the fact that the colonists had already inundated Algonquian society with English goods. He lamented that the settlers "so glutted the Salvages with their commodities as they became not regarded" (Smith et al. 1986, 1:211). Flooding native markets with European trade items violated both gift and commodity economies. It upset the English exchange system by severely disrupting the trade balance, and creating an excess in supply that almost entirely negated demand. At the same time, the native gift economy felt the ramifications of the transgression as well. Among Powhatan tribes, the inundation had eroded the bond between exchange partners and disrupted future interaction.

At first, the extended series of balanced reciprocal gift exchanges of copper for sustenance left neither group indebted to each other; the English were temporarily fed, and the natives obtained copper they could use to gain status within their indigenous tribute system. Over time this left the colonists with an ongoing need for sustenance-based exchanges, while the natives acquired increasingly larger stores of European metal scraps. This ultimately devalued the English trade goods as the natives used the copper much more slowly than the settlers consumed the food. The inundation of European trade goods led to indigenous exchange denials and hostilities.

Smith was repeatedly rebuffed during attempts to procure food through exchange with nearby indigenous tribes, forcing him to seek out other sources of food trade. In late November and December of 1607, Smith made four trading excursions into Chickahominy territory to locate untapped native exchange sources. Each of these ventures was successful. The independent merchant-like Chickahominies engaged Smith and his men in commodity exchanges without any initial gift offerings. During his voyage up the Chickahominy, Smith engaged natives at many villages, exchanging large amounts of copper and hatchets for corn. He described his dealings very simply, remarking that, "What I liked I bought" (Smith et al. 1986, 1:71). Fearing dwindling Chickahominy food surpluses, the Cape Merchant decided to travel farther upriver on his next trip to the area.

*Period IV: Abduction; December 1607*

Smith's fourth venture into Chickahominy territory was marked with violent attacks from neighboring Powhatan tribes. The mishaps of this trade venture began when a colonist disobeyed Smith's orders and went ashore near the Powhatan village of Appocant. Colonist George Cassen was "stripped naked and bound to two stakes, with his backe against a great fire, [at which point the natives] did rippe him and burne his bowels, and dried his flesh to the bones" (Smith et al. 1986, 1:175). Meanwhile, Smith, two colonists, and two Chickahominy guides faced equally antagonistic Algonquians near the village of Rassawek. A Pamunkey hunting party ambushed them, killing Jehu Robinson and Thomas Emmery and striking Smith in the thigh with an arrow. The Pamunkeys took the Cape Merchant hostage and tied him to a tree in front of a row of armed natives preparing to fire. At this moment, Smith presented Chief Opechancanough with a compass. According to Smith, the gift of the compass and his subsequent explanation of how the earth gravitated about the sun so impressed the Algonquians that they changed their mind about slaughtering him. They untied Smith and requited him with numerous gifts of food. The Pamunkeys gave Smith so much food during the next few days that he wondered if the natives "would fat him to eat him" or "intended to . . . sacrifice him" (Smith et al. 1986, 1:59, 2:148). The Algonquians then led Smith on a trek that ended at Chief Powhatan's home at Werowocomoco. Native warriors brought Smith before the Mamanatowick, and once again it appeared that his life would be sacrificed. The Algonquians forced the Cape Merchant to his knees and placed his head on a large rock as others approached with clubs in their hands "ready . . . to beat out his braines" (Smith et al. 1986, 2:151). Just as Smith's life appeared over, the Mamanatowick's "dearest daughter" Pocahontas allegedly intervened "and laid her owne [body] upon his to save him from death" (Smith et al. 1986, 2:151). Thus, Smith's life was spared twice, once through an offering from him to a native leader and a second time through an alleged native intervention.

*Period V: Adoption, Peace, and Second Inundation; January–March, 1608*

Scholars have actively debated whether Pocahontas actually saved Smith (Barbour 1970; Rountree 1990; Lemay 1992; Williamson 1992; Gleach 1996, 1997; Price 2003; Townsend 2004). Two questions surface in this discussion: (1) did Smith fabricate the rescue? and (2) did Smith misinterpret the events? Although the Cape Merchant referred to this event in only one of his many overlapping narratives regarding Jamestown, there is no reason to believe that it never happened. While Smith often exaggerated in his texts, there is no evidence that proved he outrightly lied. What is known is that the details of his Powhatan abduction, tour, and rescue parallel adoption rituals practiced in a variety of Algonquian cultures (Gleach 1997:120). In fact, the overall sequence that Smith described mirrors the stages in nearly every rite of passage, a ceremony performed to facilitate a person's change in status upon any of several highly important occasions. Anthropologists have noted these kinds of initiation rituals in all cultures. Each includes a series of events that removes an individual from one group, establishes a temporary in-between realm for the person, and then marks the entrance of the person into a different aspect of society. Gleach pinpointed these elements in Smith's particular Algonquian rite of passage: "Separation is marked by Smith's capture, the liminal phase includes the procession and redefinition ritual and ended with the rescue; the final ritual in the temple marked his incorporation" (Gleach 1997:120). Pocahontas's rescue of Smith was followed by the Mamanatowick's declaration of the English captain as his son and weroance. This marked the last phase of an extended adoption ritual that began with the initial Pamunkey abduction. In claiming that Pocahontas saved him, Smith most likely misinterpreted the Algonquian ritual, believing that the ceremonial symbolic death and transformation were actually grave threats against his life.

Chief Powhatan's ceremonial adoption of Smith served as a symbolic gesture that re-established amicable relations between the natives and the English. This adoption extended to include the Jamestown colony as part of Tsenacommacah, transforming each settler from Englishman to Anglo-Powhatan (Gleach 1997:120). The Mamanatowick's incorporation of Smith and the Jamestown settlement into Powhatan society was consistent with the rest of his tribal governance. In general, Chief Powhatan maintained his supremacy by placing his heirs as leaders of the local tribes (Gleach 1997:120). By adopting the English into the Algonquian world, the Mamanatowick secured for himself the opportunity to control and monitor the flow of English trade items into Powhatan society in the same way that he regulated the movement of tributary items in his chiefdom (Potter 1989:157). The colonists had been unwittingly adopted as tributary members of Powhatan society and, according to Algonquian norms, were now subject to indigenous rules of exchange.

The Mamanatowick finalized the social transformation of the English with a series of gifts and the establishment of future tribute payments and rewards for the colony. He promised food and peace to the settlers in exchange for hatchets and copper. Powhatan declared Smith to be "his sonne Nantaquoud" and insisted that the Cape Merchant transplant the Jamestown settlement from Paspahegh territory to the town of Capahowasick located five miles to the east of the Mamanatowick's Werowocomoco home along the north shore of the York River (Smith et al. 1986, 1:57, 2:151–152). In exchange for land, title, food, and prestige, Powhatan desired "two great gunnes [cannons], and a gryndstone" (Smith et al. 1986, 1:57, 2:151–152). Adhering to the rules of the English commodity economy, the settlers in the past had refused to exchange weapons with the Algonquians because the natives offered nothing that matched the threat of the colonists relinquishing their guns and swords. As a new member of Powhatan society, Jamestown's Cape Merchant faced a dilemma. Should he violate Algonquian rules of exchange and refuse to reciprocate or transgress English economic practices and part with European weaponry that had no material equivalent in native society for the colonists?

The Cape Merchant agreed to the Mamanatowick's requests even though he had no intention of moving the English settlement or of giving up the cannons. Instead, when Powhatan couriers came to James Fort to retrieve the cannons, he deliberately terrified them. He led the Algonquians to the guns and then fired them in the opposite direction; the blast sent the natives running for their lives. The colonists promptly searched out the bewildered Algonquians and gave them small presents to calm their nerves. Smith then "sent to Powhatan, his women, and children such presents, as gave them in generall full content" (Smith et al. 1986, 2:152). Through this strategic diversion, Smith—as he would do repeatedly—successfully avoided the predicament of clashing economic systems.

On January 2, 1608, Captain Newport returned to Jamestown with the First Supply, the initial relief mission that included fresh supplies and 100 new colonists. However, a fire broke out at James Fort just days later. Smith reported that, "by a mischaunce our Fort was burned, and the most of our apparell, lodging and private provision" (Smith et al. 1986, 1:61). The Powhatans eased the strain from the fire by providing the colonists with regular sustenance during the first few months of 1608.

The Mamanatowick sustained the Cape Merchant every other day with gifts of food. Powhatan gave Smith additional trade items as well, with the understanding that "[Smith] as their market clarke [clerk] [would] set the price how [the natives] should sell" (Smith et al. 1986, 1:215). As a result, Smith was simultaneously acting as the English Cape Merchant and Powhatan weroance. He was regulating exchange between both the colonists and the Algonquians. Things got out of his control however, and as January of 1608 came to a close, the Europeans that arrived with the First Supply began to devalue English goods by trading them to the natives in huge quantities. Smith had expressed anger at the original settlers for glutting Algonquian society with European copper two and half months earlier and had taken steps to prevent it from happening again. Nonetheless, exchange by sailors who brought the relief supplies to the Chesapeake went unchecked. Smith wrote that, "Now the arrivall of this first supply, so overjoyed us, that we could not devise too much to please the mariners. We gave them liberty to truck or trade at their pleasures. But in short time, it followed, that could not be had for a pound of copper, which before was sold for an ounce. Thus ambition, and sufferance [sanction by failing to intervene], cut the throat of our trade" (Smith et al. 1986, 1:215).

Smith also asserted that this second market inundation into Powhatan society resulted not only from seamen and new colonists but from other English leaders as well. He insisted that rival members of the Jamestown Council intentionally flooded the native world in an attempt to appear more generous and powerful than Smith. In accordance with indigenous economic goals, these Europeans attempted to gain status by giving. The Cape Merchant explained that, "the President [Ratcliffe] and Councell so much envied his [Smith's] estimation among the Salvages . . . that they wrought it into the Salvages understandings (by their great bounty in giving foure times more for their commodities then Smith appointed) that their greatnesse and authoritie as much exceeded his, as their bountie and liberalitie" (Smith et al. 1986, 1:215). This entry in the historical records documented very clearly that Smith understood the link between gift giving and the acquisition of status in Algonquian society and the economic realities of supply and demand. He resented how other English leaders jeopardized the colony's future for personal gains in prestige. During the early months of 1608, the colonists witnessed no detrimental consequences of this economic transgression. Like the effects of the previous inundation, however, interaction would soon become strained and ultimately violent.

### Period VI: Deteriorating Relations; March–June, 1608

The inundation of indigenous villages with European exchange items, in conjunction with the colonists' failure to move their settlement to Capahowasick, dissolved the English/Powhatan bond and led to theft and violence during the spring of 1608. By April of 1608, Smith noted and lamented rampant native theft, writing that the Powhatans were taking anything they could seize. He suggested that the Mamanatowick sanctioned these thefts, observing that, "what others can steale, their King receiveth" (Smith et al. 1986, 1:215). Chief Powhatan did not tolerate theft between his subjects. He did, however, permit his Algonquian followers to pilfer the goods of non-Powhatans (Rountree 1993:179). The Mamanatowick's approval of stealing from the English suggested that he no longer considered the colonists as part of his chiefdom. Smith and his comrades had been disowned.

Two exchange-system violations by the settlers—both with elapsing time limits—distanced, alienated, and antagonized the Powhatans. The colonists did not move their settlement to Capahowasick as the Mamanatowick had requested. This meant that they had refused a gift of land from Chief Powhatan. The Mamanatowick emphasized this denial when comparing the two English captains with whom he interacted the most—Smith and Newport. Chief Powhatan declared that, "Newport . . . [was] ever taking what I offred him, but not [Smith]" (Smith et al. 1986, 1:248). Smith continuously resided at Jamestown from 1607 to 1609 whereas Newport visited the American colony only sporadically. Powhatan's complaints focused on daily interaction with Smith as opposed to infrequent and largely ceremonial meetings with Newport. Smith's refusals not only upset Algonquian economic norms, they also disrupted the social hierarchy. No indigenous weroance dared to refuse a gift from Chief Powhatan. The English failure to move was a social insult that undermined the Mamanatowick's authority. If Chief Powhatan did not punish this affront, other subjects might reject his offerings and alliance and question his authority as well.

In addition, the second inundation of native society with European goods decreased overall interaction. As before, a few weeks after Smith noticed the economic glut, relations deteriorated and soon afterward, violence erupted. With the established Powhatan link between status, prestigious goods, and gift exchange, flooding indigenous society violated the native economy in a second way. Like all participants in the commodity-exchange system, the English privileged the items transferred above the relationships forged with their indigenous exchange partners. They sought food and traded copper to Powhatans regardless of status. The colonists' distribution of the key Algonquian spiritual good was arbitrary. Instead of elite natives controlling the movement of prestigious goods, lesser Algonquians now acquired these socially powerful items. The English economic violations were a social slap in the face of the Mamanatowick and his weroances, the most powerful Algonquians in the Chesapeake.

A few days before Newport left for England on April 22, 1608, Chief Powhatan "presented him with 20 Turkies, conditionally to returne him 20 swords" (Smith et al. 1986, 1:220). This transaction stood out from other exchanges as a gift/commodity hybrid. Although it fulfilled many criteria of the gift economy —the exchange was between individuals of similar status who had interacted before and would continue to engage one another in a friendly manner—the Mamanatowick made the implicit return offering entirely explicit. In the past, gifts had been made and requited but never were the return gifts specified in advance (with the exception of the cannons that Smith avoided giving). Furthermore, Chief Powhatan emphasized the conditionality of the initial offering. Conditionality revealed a lack of trust. That the Mamanatowick felt the need to clarify gift-exchange rules to the English implied that the colonists had not been adequately following these standards. The one-to-one ratio of turkeys to swords also underscored an equation of material exchange values uncommon to Algonquian trade norms. This transaction spotlighted the goods involved in the exchange, not the bond between Newport and Powhatan. The English transfer of weapons was uncharacteristic as well. In few other instances did the settlers release arms to the natives. The threat of strengthening the Powhatans was not offset by the value of any indigenous exchange good. Newport, however, ignored the commodity-based requirements of obtaining equivalent return items and provided the Mamanatowick with weapons. Just as the alienated Powhatans distanced themselves from gift exchange with the settlers, the English captain softened commodity-based restrictions.

Overall, English relations with the Powhatans continued to worsen. On April 26, 1608, a group of Paspaheghs attempted to ambush Smith and colonist Mathew Scrivener outside of the fort. The two colonists narrowly avoided the trap and hurried back to their settlement. The natives followed, pretending to have other business with the English. They told the Cape Merchant that they knew of a native spy who resided at James Fort and "offered to beat him" (Smith et al. 1986, 1:87). As he listened to their explanation, Smith casually drew the Paspaheghs inside of the palisaded compound and then abruptly "shut the Ports [gates], and apprehended them" (Smith et al. 1986, 1:87). With the added leverage of hostages, the colonists sent word to their Algonquian neighbors that if the natives did not return all stolen English property by the next day, the captives would be executed. The Paspaheghs retaliated by taking two English men prisoner. In response, Smith abducted additional Algonquians.

The Paspaheghs released their English captives, "desir[ing] peace without any farther composition [terms or compensation] for their prisoners" (Smith et al. 1986, 1:89). The English acknowledged the native gesture by setting one native free, but they kept the other hostages. Smith questioned the remaining captives as to who instructed them to assault the settlers. After being tortured, the Algonquians confessed to Smith that Chief Powhatan had ordered the attack and specified that he wanted the colonists to be killed with their own weapons. Reminiscent of Don Luis's attack on the Jesuits in 1571, the Powhatans attempted to acquire English arms and use them, instead of traditional native weaponry, against the colonists. The captives listed the Algonquian tribes that joined in the plan against the settlers, including the Paspahegh, the Chickahominy, Youghtanunds, Pamunkey, Mattaponi, and Kiskiacks. The Youghtanunds and Mattaponi likely joined in trading ventures with the English at Pamunkey, and the Kiskiacks were probably part of the exchanges days earlier at nearby Werowocomoco. Whereas the first large-scale indigenous attack against the Jamestown colonists was championed by Powhatan groups who had been angered by English failures to reciprocate, tribes that had either been denied reciprocity or inundated by the settlers undertook this round of native hostility.

Once the hostages revealed the Powhatan conspiracy to destroy Jamestown, indigenous leaders apologized and attempted to secure peace with gifts. The colonists countered with presents of their own. The mutual offerings tentatively re-established amicable relations between the groups. The Mamanatowick immediately sent Pocahontas to Jamestown with "a Deere and bread" for Smith, attempting "to excuse . . . the injuries done by his subjects, desiring their liberties, [and] with the assurance of his love for ever" (Smith et al. 1986, 1:89, 91, 220). Likewise, Opechancanough "sent [Smith] his shooting Glove and Bracer [wrist guard] . . . in token of peace" (Smith et al. 1986, 1:93, 95). After receiving these presents, the English gave the hostages to Pocahontas and offered her trifles.

## Period VII: Chesapeake Exploration; June–August, 1608

Smith led a small crew on repeated missions to explore the northern Chesapeake Bay in the summer of 1608 (Rountree and Davidson 1997:48). Many of the tribes along the eastern shore, following orders of the Mamanatowick, met the English with immediate hostility. Smith repeatedly countered native animus with a display of strength and then gift offerings, attempting to emphasize the Europeans' formidability and generosity. This sequence frequently made allies out of enemies. Chief Powhatan's scheme paralleled Pemisipan's unsuccessful 1586 attempt at killing Lane and his men by sending them into hostile Chawanoac territory. Smith's military might and prestigious trade goods undermined the Mamanatowick's attempts to have other Chesapeake tribes eliminate the English. Early in the summer of 1608, Smith formed an alliance with Mannahoacks and Massawomecks, both adversaries of the Mamanatowick and his followers. The English presented many prestigious goods to these tribes, some of the same items that the colonists had withheld from certain Powhatan groups in the past. By privileging the Mamanatowick's rivals, the colonists further diminished relations with Chief Powhatan and his people.

On one of the voyages back to the fort, Smith grabbed a stingray with his bare hand and was severely injured. His upper torso swelled enormously, and most of the crew thought that he would not survive the trip back to their compound. Fortunately for Smith, the expedition team included Doctor Walter Rusell, who nursed him back to health. Smith returned to Jamestown on September 7, 1608, to a diseased and disgruntled colony. He wrote that, "We safely arrived . . . [and] found . . . many dead; some sicke: the late President [Ratcliffe] prisoner for mutiny, . . . [and] the provision in the store much spoyled with rayne" (Smith et al. 1986, 2:180). Three days later, the Jamestown council elected Smith as president.

## Period VIII: Third Inundation; September, 1608–January, 1609

During the fall of 1608, the colonists again flooded native society with European exchange goods. Native rejections of the settlers' attempts at trade dominated this period and foreshadowed impending violence. Around the same time, Newport returned to the settlement with the Second Supply. Along with additional colonists and provisions, he carried a letter from the London Council that scolded Jamestown's settlers for the lack of progress in becoming self-sufficient.

Virginia Company officials insisted that Newport immediately crown the Mamanatowick as a vassal of King James I. Smith and a few of his men ventured to Werowocomoco in October of 1608 to invite Chief Powhatan to their fort for the ceremony. The Mamanatowick mistrusted the offer and insisted that the coronation be held at his home village. Newport ultimately presided at the official ceremony for the English and offered the indigenous leader "presents of Bason, Ewer, Bed, Bedstead, Clothes, and [other] such costly novelties" (Smith et al. 1986. 2:184). Chief Powhatan would not don the "scarlet Cloake [the Newport offered him] . . . [until] being perswaded [that it] . . . would not hurt him" (Smith et al. 1986, 2:184). Newport intended to place the copper headdress on the Mamanatowick, but Powhatan refused to "kneele to receive [the] Crowne" (Smith et al. 1986, 2:184). After much effort that "tyred them all," the colonists encouraged the native leader to bow by "leaning hard on his shoulders," allowing Newport a brief moment to crown the Mamanatowick while "he a little stooped" (Smith et al. 1986, 2:184). The slight head bob was as close to an elaborate reverent bow as the settlers were going to get out of Chief Powhatan. When an English boat fired a cannon to celebrate the completion of the ritual, the Mamanatowick "start[ed] up in a horrible feare," believing that the colonists had launched an attack (Smith et al. 1986, 2:184).

Smith reflected negatively on the coronation, declaring that these gifts from Newport made Powhatan believe that he deserved more from the colonists on a regular basis. He reported that the goods given during the ceremony were ill spent because they "made [the Mamanatowick] so much overvalue himselfe, that he respected us as much as nothing at all" (Smith et al. 1986, 2:181). Smith also pinpointed the third devaluation of English goods at Jamestown, noting that, "we had his favour much better onely for a playne peece of Copper, till this stately kind of soliciting" (Smith et al. 1986, 2:181). Chief Powhatan requited Newport for the elaborate ceremonial gifts with "his old shoes and his mantle" (Smith et al. 1986, 2:184).

Instead of these gift transactions bolstering the bond between exchange partners, they demonstrated the growing distance between the two groups. The Mamanatowick was suspicious of the ceremony, refused to kneel, and offered little to the English as compensation. Not only did Smith believe that this coronation devalued English goods, he also fretted about the settlers, especially individuals who had just arrived in the Chesapeake, further flooding Powhatan society with English items. The inundation undermined trade, violated commodity economics, and diminished the long-range future of their colony. Smith pinpointed the Jamestown tavern as an active market with "damnable and private trade" that was independent of his supervision and control (Smith et al. 1986, 2:186). He lamented that, "any thing [the colonists] could steale from their fellowes was vendible . . . with the Salvages" (Smith et al. 1986, 2:187).

Ignoring the intricate details and events leading up to the Mamanatowick's coronation might lead one to deduce that this elaborate ceremony consisted of amicable gift exchanges between allies. The celebrated events included two elite individuals who had transacted before and would transact again. They presented each other with something-for-nothing offerings. The form of the exchange and the bond and status of the exchange partners would suggest that the transaction further linked these two groups already bonded by gift giving. However, close inspection of the surrounding circumstances exposed this ceremony as a microcosm of failing English/Powhatan relations. Instead of a gift exchange that signified acceptance, this transaction embodied refusal. The Mamanatowick rejected the colonists' offer to host the ceremony and refused to place a crown atop his head. In addition, Chief Powhatan's reciprocation consisted of flagrantly insufficient return goods—used shoes and an old cloak. The English had again devalued their trade goods and alienated the indigenous population. As a result, the Mamanatowick abandoned gift-exchange norms that emphasized and enabled the acquisition of debt. On the contrary, he initiated efforts to profit off of the alienated colonists.

Immediately following Powhatan's coronation, the colonists endured an extended series of native denials. The settlers often responded with violence. The Powhatans rejected English offers to conquer the Monacans. Furthermore, on Smith's next trade expedition he encountered natives who "refus[ed] to trade, with as much scorne and insolency as they could expresse" (Smith et al. 1986, 2:186). The English held the Mamanatowick responsible for this embargo, suggesting that he had implemented a policy to starve the colonists. Jamestown's president sent colonist Matthew Scrivener with some men to Werowocomoco on a trading mission and found the Algonquians "more ready to fight than trade" (Smith et al. 1986, 2:187). Smith himself went to Nansamund in search of food, but the natives denied him, insisting that the Mamanatowick had "commanded [them] to keepe that [which] they had, and not to let [the colonists] come into their river" (Smith et al. 1986, 2:191). The settlers attempted to trade with other natives, but the Powhatan collectively avoided the English.

When Newport left the colony for England on December 1, 1608, he carried with him a bitter written response from Smith to the Virginia Company regarding their criticisms of the settlement's progress. With dwindling food stores dangerously low, Smith instituted a new colony law linking the diligence and the sustenance of individuals at Jamestown. Frustrated by what he perceived as laziness on the part of many settlers and now holding substantial power and seniority, Smith mandated that, "he that will not worke shall not eat" (Smith et al. 1986, 1:259).

### Period IX: Assassination Attempts; January–August, 1609

Failing to fulfill gift-exchange obligations and flooding native society with European copper for a third time contributed to numerous indigenous attacks during the first half of 1609. When Smith informed Chief Powhatan that he came to trade on January 13, 1609, the Mamanatowick offered him 40 baskets of native corn for 40 swords. Chief Powhatan's desires had clearly changed. He no longer wanted copper, and in its place he requested weapons. The Mamanatowick declared that when it came to English "Commodities, . . . none he liked [except] gunnes and swordes" (Smith et al. 1986, 2:194). This switch in the identity of the goods that the Algonquians most desired had severe ramifications. It prevented opposite exchange violations from minimizing each other. The English simultaneously flooded native society and failed to give and reciprocate adequately. They both offered too much and too little. The colonists had devalued copper while also failing to provide other items that the Algonquians wanted, especially weapons. Even though the Powhatans no longer desired English copper, they nonetheless merited return gifts for the presents they had previously offered to the settlers. Chief Powhatan pointed out the devaluation of European trade goods by reminding Smith that native exchange items served a practical purpose—they eased hunger—and the English offerings did not. Reversing the traditional gift-economy priority on the individuals involved in the transaction rather than the material value of the goods, the Mamanatowick asserted that, "he could eat his Corne, but not the copper" (Smith et al. 1986, 2:194). With relations severely strained between alienated natives and colonists, Chief Powhatan now prized the utility of the trade items above the social link between the people involved in the exchange. According to the indigenous population, an English/Algonquian bond no longer existed. The two groups had again become aliens.

Smith confronted the Mamanatowick regarding indigenous attempts at starving the English. He reminded Chief Powhatan that the settlers could take native food by force, stating that, "[English] swordes, and gunnes . . . can keep me from want [of food]" (Smith et al. 1986, 2:194). Smith emphasized, however, that he chose not to "dissolve [their] friendship" (Smith et al. 1986, 2:195). As president of the Jamestown Council, Smith declared that Chief Powhatan's embargo and "bad usage" of the colonists transgressed gift-based bonds (Smith et al. 1986, 2:195). During his speech to the Mamanatowick, he alluded to the characteristics that defined the Algonquian economy, referring to "gifts . . . [that] gain more then by trade" and "curtesies . . . [not being] a vendible commodity" (Smith et al. 1986, 1:249). Ironically, Smith clung to native gift-exchange rules just as Chief Powhatan switched to a commodity-economy mindset when dealing with the English. Jamestown's president moved away from commodity-based exchange protocol in a similar manner as Newport had done in April of 1608 when he agreed to trade swords for turkeys. Both of these economic compromises by English leaders preceded indigenous attacks by days. Their actions were desperate attempts at reversing exchange-based transgressions that had already alienated and antagonized the natives to the point of violent retribution.

Following Smith's pleas, Chief Powhatan duplicitously agreed to give the colonists food when it arrived from the interior and implied that he had lifted the embargo. Yet, the Mamanatowick had no intention of fulfilling these promises and used them only to lull Smith into a false sense of security. While the English waited for corn to be delivered, Jamestown's president traded with the Mamanatowick, getting "ten quarters of Corne for a copper Kettel" (Smith et al. 1986, 2:195). Smith knew that this exchange rate did not favor the English and, as a result, demanded more corn from the following year's crop. Ignoring Smith's demand and just moments before the Powhatans launched an attack at Smith and his crew, the Mamanatowick revealed his lethal motives. He informed the English of their many socioeconomic violations that had alienated the Chesapeake Algonquians and provoked their violent wrath. Chief Powhatan identified Smith's refusals to give and reciprocate with adequate items, telling him that, "I never use any Werowance so kindely as your selfe, yet from you I receive the least kindnesse of any . . . I seek to content you . . . [yet] I can have nothing but what you regard not" (Smith et al. 1986, 2:195). The Mamanatowick saw Smith's Cape-Merchant decisions for the colony as unkind gestures. Since the Algonquians failed to separate gift exchange and emotion, the English actions were personal affronts as well as economic violations. In a system that unites the giver, the spirit of the giver, the act of giving, and the gift itself, exchange and emotion are inextricably linked. The Mamanatowick asserted that Smith failed to behave like a weroance in other ways as well, remarking that, "none doth deny to lye at my feet, or refuse to doe what I desire, but onely you" (Smith et al. 1986, 2:195). These transgressions, combined with the overall devalued English presence in the Chesapeake due to repeated economic inundation, prompted extended hostilities.

At this point, the Mamanatowick ordered a few of his followers to break the ice that covered the shore of the York River as a favor for Smith, but this false gift immediately preceded an attack. Smith and his men had momentarily retired to a nearby Algonquian house. Secretly, Chief Powhatan had ordered his armed men to attack them. Smith anticipated the native attack, opened fire when the Algonquians entered the building, and quelled the assault. In an effort to improve severely diminished English/Algonquian relations, Smith left a few of his men at Werowocomoco to construct a house for Chief Powhatan (Smith et al. 1986, 2:199).

Jamestown's president had successfully engineered alliances in the past by countering native violence with a display of strength and subsequent gift offerings. This time, however, his plan backfired. Hours after the English left Werowocomoco, Chief Powhatan sent the disgruntled colonists Smith left behind to Jamestown Island to obtain weapons for the natives. These settlers not only obtained many weapons, they also recruited six additional defectors. Smith's gifts had opportunistic and traitorous minds of their own.

Smith and his crew entered Pamunkey territory on January 16, 1609. Chief Opechancanough promptly feasted the English visitors. Algonquians again used false gifts to lure the colonists into an ambush. The indigenous leader had successfully baited the colonists into a native house surrounded by more than 700 armed warriors. Then Opechancanough duplicitously offered Smith "a great present at the doore," in an attempt to draw him out into the open area where each Pamunkey warrior had "his arrow nocked [and] ready to shoot" (Smith et al. 1986, 2:201). Smith abruptly snatched the Pamunkey leader by the head, put his pistol against Opechancanough's chest, and dragged him out the door by his hair. Jamestown's president ordered the warriors to lower their weapons, which they immediately did. Smith then reminded the Pamunkeys of their previous promise to fill his ship with corn. He vowed that if they kept their word, their weroance would suffer no harm; if they did not, Smith pledged to "load [his vessel] with . . . [Pamunkey] carcasses" (Smith et al. 1986, 2:202). The Pamunkeys filled the English ship, prompting Smith to free Opechancanough.

When the English team left Pamunkey, they sailed down the York River and passed by Werowocomoco. Chief Powhatan's followers again attempted to deceive the colonists, enticing the English with empty promises of gifts. Smith insisted on bringing armed escorts ashore, which caused the Algonquians to rescind their offers. What appeared to be an ambush in the making resulted in the exchange of neither blood nor gifts. Overall, the natives repeatedly used false gifts to deceive the English during this period.

The only indigenous group to maintain consistent trade relations with the settlers during their first year and a half at Jamestown Island was the Chickahominies, the lone Algonquian group that embraced a commodity mindset. The merchant ways of the Chickahominies corresponded with English economic expectations, as opposed to the gift mindset of the other Powhatan groups. Yet even English/Chickahominy relations were strained during the late summer of 1609. When a Chickahominy youth stole a pistol, Smith "apprehended two proper young [indigenous] fellowes, that were brothers, known to be confederates" of the thief (Smith et al. 1986, 2:202). He imprisoned one, and "the other was sent to returne the Pistoll . . . within twelve hours, or his brother [would] be hanged" (Smith et al. 1986, 2:202). While they waited, Smith gave his hostage some food and charcoal for a fire. The captive's brother appeared at James Fort around midnight with the pistol. When the English went to retrieve the native's sibling, Smith noted that they discovered "the poore Salvage in the dungeon . . . so smothered with the smoake he had made, and so pittiously burnt, that wee found him dead" (Smith et al. 1986, 2:202).

*Period X: Resuscitation; August–September, 1609*

As the prisoner lay motionless on the dungeon floor, Smith made an offer to the victim's brother. Jamestown's president promised "that if hereafter [all Algonquians] would not steale [from the English], he wold make [the native's sibling] alive again" (Smith et al. 1986, 2:202). The Chickahominy youth agreed to these terms, and Smith, "with Aqua vitae [liquor] and Vinegar . . . restored him againe to life" (Smith et al. 1986, 2:202). The resuscitation led to successive gift exchanges and the re-establishment of an alliance between the colonists and Algonquians. With both of the Chickahominy brothers alive and well and the stolen pistol returned to its English owner, Smith rewarded the two natives for their cooperation by giving each a piece of copper. They left the fort that day with small tokens of English gratitude and a story "that . . . was spread among all the Salvages for a miracle" of how "Captaine Smith could make a man alive that was dead" (Smith et al. 1986, 2:202). The rumor of Smith's seemingly supernatural ability "amazed and affrighted both [Chief] Powhatan, and all his people" (Smith et al. 1986, 2:202). The previous chapter discussed Algonquian reverence of individuals with the power to rejuvenate themselves and others, perceived as an "infusion of godliness" (Strachey 1953:60–61). It also critiqued yet another Western depiction of indigenous reverence. Both discussions are relevant here as well. Upon hearing of Smith's otherworldly talent, natives from all over the region offered gifts and desired peace, prompting Jamestown's president to remark that, "all the Country became . . . free for us" (Smith et al. 1986, 2:211). Gift exchange and its system of seemingly free offerings once again became the norm for intercultural transactions.

*Period XI: Smith's Departure and War; September, 1609–1611*

After reading Smith's acerbic response to their previous administrative admonishment, Virginia Company leaders in England restructured the colonial venture in the Chesapeake, demoted the irreverent Smith, and named Thomas Gates as lieutenant governor. A hurricane wrecked the ship that carried Gates and some of the other prominent new colonists at Bermuda in July of 1609. The rest of the Third Supply arrived without incident in the Chesapeake. Thus, the new charter announced the administrative changes, but because of the stranded leaders, was unable to enact them.

Smith ignored the new charter's instructions and named Captain John Martin as his successor. Martin, however, resigned as Council President and took 100 men to Nansamund with the intention of establishing a new English outpost. His crew split into two groups. Martin's lieutenant headed the first, which traveled by land, and Martin and Percy guided the second, which went by water. Once there, Martin dispatched two of his men to bargain with the Nansamund weroance for the purchase of a nearby island. Instead of entertaining the offer that Martin's men made, the natives killed the English messengers and "cutt and skraped [their brains] outt of their heades with mussell shelles" (Percy 1967:263). In an attempt to avenge his comrades, Martin's lieutenant led an attack on the Nansamunds. The English "Beate the Salvages outt of the Island, burned their howses, Ransaked their Temples, [and] Tooke downe the Corpses of their deade Kings from their Toambes [tombs]" (Percy 1967:263). Meanwhile, Martin's contingency had stirred up trouble with the natives as well. They had seized the weroance's son and accidentally shot him. The Nansamunds responded by killing Martin and his men.

Every series of interaction between the English and the Nansamunds from 1607 to 1609 began with hostility, regardless of the status of overall English relations with the Powhatans. In April of 1607, the Nansamunds led an unprovoked attack on the colonists. A year later, the settlers assaulted the Nansamunds for this initial hostility and then worked out a trade alliance. Nansamund animosity again turned to eventual amicability with the colonists in August of 1608. Four months later, Nansamunds antagonized the English, engaged in violence, and then traded. The events of September 1609 continued the pattern of initial hostility, which was exclusive to English/Nansamund interaction. With this pattern in mind, the Nansamund attacks on Martin's men were not anomalous; it was the English response that strayed from the norm. Their destruction of the native temples and tombs altered the usual sequence of events. In the past, the settlers—Smith in particular—had met Nansamund violence with a show of strength and then offers of an exchange-based resolution. The extreme nature of the English demolition of a native spiritual center eliminated the option of a peaceful economic compromise.

Following Martin's unsuccessful expedition, Captain Francis West took over 100 men up the James River to settle near the Fall Zone. Smith visited West's colony and fretted over its location because the settlement was constantly flooding. He determined that West's men needed a new place to build their outpost, contacted the Mamanatowick, and asked to purchase the town of Powhatan at the western edge of Algonquian territory. Smith guaranteed that the English would defend the Powhatans against the Monacans and pay a certain amount of copper in exchange for the village, power to punish any native who stole from the English, and annual Algonquian tribute to King James. Furthermore, Smith made an attempt to prevent the devaluation of English goods by establishing a set intercultural exchange rate, equating a bushel of corn with a square inch of copper. Henry Spelman, a young English colonist who had just arrived in the Chesapeake, declared that Smith included an additional good in this exchange, asserting that, "[Smith] sold me . . . for a towne called Powhatan" (Spelman 1872:9).

New colonists that came to Virginia with the Third Supply quickly upset the peace at West's new settlement at the town of Powhatan. These settlers "tormented those poor soules [the natives], by stealing their corne, robbing their gardens, beating them, breaking their houses and keeping some prisoners" (Smith et al. 1986, 2:222). The hostilities warranted punishment, yet many Algonquians continued to bring in their contribution to Smith and endured these atrocities (Smith et al. 1986, 2:222). As soon as Smith left for Jamestown, however, the natives ceased to tolerate these slights. The Algonquians "assaulted those hundred and twentie in their Fort [at Powhatan], finding some stragling abroad in the woods: they slew many, and so affrighted the rest" (Smith et al. 1986, 2:222). Smith immediately returned to the ravaged English outpost and attempted to repair relations. He appeased the natives by returning their stolen goods and replacing the colonial officers who oversaw the settlement.

In early October of 1609, a gunpowder explosion severely injured Smith and forced him to return to England. His departure set off a series of native attacks, "for the Salvages no sooner understood [that] Smith was gone, but they all revolted, and did spoile and murder all they incountered" (Smith et al. 1986,

2:231–232). Smith, the elite English exchange partner of the Powhatans, had established interpersonal bonds with the Mamanatowick and the lesser weroances through many gift exchanges despite intermittent frictions. Furthermore, the natives esteemed his purported life-saving ability. When Smith left, the English lost their main link to the indigenous population. The removal of a high-status intercultural liaison left a gap in the gift system. As soon as Smith sailed out of the Chesapeake, the alliance between the two groups ended and hostilities began. Third Supply settlers and their abuses of the indigenous population, combined with the departure of Smith, led to repeated violence and the extended hostilities. Thus began the First Anglo-Powhatan War (Fausz 1985, 1990).

Chief Powhatan used Spelman and duplicitous gift offerings to lure the English into an ambush. He sent Spelman to tell the colonists that "if they would bring ther ship, and some copper, [the Mamanatowick] would fraught her backe with corne" (Spelman 1872:10). Captain John Radcliffe and 25 colonists visited Orapakes, the new Powhatan capital, received gifts of food from Chief Powhatan, requited with copper and beads, and traded English copper for corn (Spelman 1872:10–11). As they traded, the colonists witnessed the natives "dealing deceitfully" by "beareing up the bottom of their baskets with their hands soe that less corne might serve to fill them" (Spelman 1872:11). In anger, the English gathered their goods and headed toward their boat. As they approached their vessel, the English saw that armed warriors now blanketed the area. Spelman declared that "before their coming" the Mamanatowick had "layd plotts to take [the colonists]" (Spelman 1872:11). The Powhatans opened fire and killed all but two of them.

Symbolic Powhatan actions again immediately preceded an indigenous slaughter of colonizing Europeans. If the Mamanatowick intended all along to eliminate Radcliffe and his men at Orapakes—as Spelman affirmed—why begin with false gift giving? Why then engineer trades that showcased deliberate mis-measurement? As before, Chesapeake Algonquians used anomalous exchanges to set the stage for their punishments of individuals who had repeatedly violated socioeconomic norms. In this case, the Powhatans added a new twist. They used unfair commodity exchanges to frustrate the English and drive them from a duplicitous bartering table into the ambush. Deriding the English emphasis on and manipulation of exchange prices, the natives' symbol-laden actions immediately foreshadowed their assault.

Algonquian antagonism increased during this time as they assaulted any colonists who left the fort. The Powhatans successfully isolated the settlers and prevented them from acquiring food. Whereas only eight settlers died during the winter of 1608–09, the subsequent "Starving Time" of November 1609 to

March 1610 saw the demise of 143 colonists, over half of the English population at Jamestown Island (Fausz 1990:55). Smith's *Proceedings* . . . detailed dire conditions that led to English cannibalism. It reported that, "so great was our famine, that a Salvage we slew, and buried, the poorer sort tooke him up again and [ate] him. . . . And one amongst the rest [of the colonists] did kill his wife, powdered her, and had eaten part of her before it was knowne, for which hee was executed" (Smith et al. 1986, 1:275–276; 2:232–233).

Previously shipwrecked Thomas Gates and his crew left Bermuda for Virginia on May 10, 1610. They arrived at Old Point Comfort 11 days later on two boats that they had constructed during the preceding months. Gates and his men then traveled to James Fort. The few supplies that Gates brought saved the ravaged colony. Seeing the disastrous conditions at Jamestown, Gates decided that the colonists should abandon their settlement. As a result, they left the three-year-old colony and sailed down the James River toward the mouth of the Chesapeake. Once in the bay, the settlers encountered a ship led by Sir Thomas West that had just completed its voyage from England. As the newly designated First Governor and Captain-General of Virginia, West—also known as Lord De La Warr—sternly ordered Gates and his followers to return to the fort, which they immediately did.

On June 10, 1610, De La Warr came ashore and assumed his official post. He enacted martial law, declared war on the indigenous population, and banned intercultural commerce (Fausz 1990:55). Following the rules and ideas in William Strachey's *Lawes Divine, Morall, and Martial,* the new Virginia governor "prohibit[ed all] . . . forms of contact between colonists and Powhatans," except warfare (Fausz 1990:31). The penalty for trading with the natives was death (Strachey 1953:15). De La Warr deliberately and immediately initiated hostility with the natives. English assaults and raids during the summer of 1610 and beyond fulfilled two of De La Warr's goals, weakening the Algonquians and securing large amounts of native corn for the English (Fausz 1990:34). Two years of consistent hostilities followed, ending with the English capture and ransom of Pocahontas. The marriage of Pocahontas to settler John Rolfe by the Reverend Richard Buck in 1614 secured a temporary peace, ending the constant hostilities that typified the late 1609 to 1612 time span.

## Jamestown Exchange Patterns

Almost all of the contact-period Powhatan attacks on the Jamestown colonists immediately followed English economic violations. The settlers' failure to reward the Paspaheghs for their many gifts distanced these natives. The colonists further provoked the alienated Paspaheghs by privileging their tribute rivals, leading to a violent attack. Other Powhatan tribes, like the Arrohattocs, Pamunkeys, and Weanocks, received prestigious items as compensation from the settlers. In return, Paspaheghs and non-Paspaheghs made similar offerings to the colonists, yet the English shunned the former and requited the latter. This denial humiliated the Paspaheghs and incited their vengeance.

Three separate English inundations of Powhatan society, combined with additional colonial violations of the native gift system, spurred consequent Algonquian assaults. In each case, the glut of European trade goods led to a month or two of native exchange rejections and thefts, followed by violence a month later. This exact sequence occurred three times at Jamestown from 1607 to 1609 (Table 5.1). Smith's adamant frustrations with unauthorized trade by new colonists led him ultimately to order the building of an 80-foot-wide garrison on the isthmus between Jamestown and the mainland in the spring of 1609. Its primary purpose was to prevent unauthorized intercultural exchange (Quitt 1995:243; Barbour 1964:147–148, 210–211, 279–280).

Each of the three sets of violence that followed the economic inundations was of different intensity. The Mamanatowick's role in each of the hostile acts varied as well. The first assaults in December of 1607 consisted of two isolated attacks, one on Smith and his small crew, and the other on a lone settler who left the barge at Appocant. Contemporary sources minimized Chief Powhatan's part in these two assaults. The second group of skirmishes in April of 1608 consisted of an ambush on Smith and Scrivener, Paspahegh abductions of two English settlers, and the Mamanatowick's conspiracy to attack James Fort. It also included Chief Powhatan's attempt to have Smith and his men killed by the indigenous population while they explored the Chesapeake. In this case, the Mamanatowick planned the demise of the colonists, but he took no active role in it. The third set of assaults in early 1609 included repeated Powhatan, Pamunkey, and Paspahegh ambushes. The natives lured the English into these traps with false gifts. Chief Powhatan was more active in this set of attacks than the previous two. He spearheaded many of these assaults, personally baiting the colonists.

These differing intensities of the native attacks, as well as the degree of the Mamanatowick's involvement, corresponded with specific aspects of the economic violations committed by the English (Table 5.2). No gift-exchange transgressions accompanied the colonists' first inundation of native society. The second glut of European goods was joined by the settlers' failure to accept Chief Powhatan's offer to move James Fort to Capahowasick. As the colonists flooded the native world for the third time, settlement leaders failed to give and recip-

Table 5.1. Pattern of inundation, date of theft or trade rejections, and date of violence

| Inundation number | Identity of settlers who flooded the market | Date of inundation | Date of thefts or trade rejections | Date of violence |
|---|---|---|---|---|
| First | Original colonists | October 1607 | November 1607 | December 1607 |
| Second | First Supply colonists | January 1608 | March 1608 | April 1608 |
| Third | Second Supply colonists | October/ November 1608 | October– December 1608 | January 1609 |

Table 5.2. Pattern of inundation and Mamanatowick involvement in hostilities against the English settlers

| Inundation number | Other English exchange violations | Degree of hostility | Mamanatowick's involvement in the violence |
|---|---|---|---|
| First | None | Isolated attack | Little if any |
| Second | Failure to accept | Single plot with multiple attacks | Secondhand; directed violence covertly and from afar |
| Third | Failure to give, Failure to reciprocate, Exchange with rivals after failure to reciprocate | Widespread antagonism with constant strife | Firsthand; directed violence openly and from close proximity |

rocate adequately. They also engaged and established alliances with Powhatan enemies, such as the Mannahoacks and Massawomecks. Thus, in Algonquian society there was a link between the attack, those involved, namely Chief Powhatan, and the number and type of economic transgressions.

The last set of intercultural violence, from fall 1609 through 1611, began when members of the Third Supply repeatedly antagonized the indigenous population. Hostility toward an exchange partner violated the gift economy and warranted retribution. The Algonquians endured these slights as long as Smith remained at the settlement. Yet, as soon as Smith left the Chesapeake, the natives began to attack the colonists. The removal of an elite gift-exchange partner, especially one with a purportedly divine talent, eroded the alliance between the groups. With no intercultural liaison and growing English abuse of the Algonquians, widespread native aggression soon erupted.

## Jamestown Post-Script

The significant and symbolic link between exchange and violence does not end in the Anglo/Powhatan Chesapeake following the extended conflicts from 1610 to 1613. In fact, violence and exchange secured the peace. The English kidnapping and ransoming of Pocahontas and her subsequent marriage to colonist John Rolfe marked a temporary end to the intercultural hostilities. Symbol-laden violence continued to play an important role as well. For example, the Algonquians carefully choreographed their 1622 uprising by using European tools and weapons to annihilate a quarter of the English colony. In addition, the colonists were nearly successful in murdering the Mamanatowick Opechancanough with a false gift of poisoned wine in 1623 (Fausz 1977:498; Rountree 1990:77).

However, the nature of the historical record for the colony changes following the 1610–13 conflicts. What was once a detailed inventory of interaction that can be effectively reconstructed for a reliable microchronology of events becomes a set of isolated accounts of exceptional historical occurrences (See Quitt 1995). Analysis of these more segmented events requires a different methodological technique than the one explained, defended, and employed here. As a result, post-1613 Jamestown events fall outside the scope of this study.

# 6
## *Conclusion*

Europeans and Algonquians maintained different motivations and tactics in their political and socioeconomic dealings with one another. In the course of discussing their differences, this analysis has endeavored to show how socioeconomic violations were one of a handful of likely catalysts for conflict. Exchange was not *the* cause of aggression between the Algonquians and Europeans at Ajacan, Roanoke, and Jamestown; it was *a* cause, one that was showcased symbolically in Algonquian violence and substantiated in the chronological details of the early colonial records. In addition, anthropological models of exchange isolated cultural exchange norms for these contact-period natives, colonists, and missionaries. Previously discussed categories of exchange form, exchange-partner relationship, and exchange-item alienation helped to define the nature and practice of each system.

## Elite Euro-Algonquian Exchange

When engaging European settlers, Carolina and Chesapeake Algonquian leaders followed a gift economy. Nearly every economic criterion Marcel Mauss identified in his model was evident in elite Algonquian exchange practices. These natives regularly initiated exchanges that maintained a superficial something-for-nothing form, even though they were actually something-for-nothing now in exchange for something-for-nothing later. They also kept transactions between individuals of like status, made successful attempts at acquiring debt as opposed to material wealth, emphasized interpersonal bonds over the utility of the goods, put a premium on accruing debt as opposed to obtaining immediate material profit, and accused colonists of gift-exchange violations.

*Something-for-Nothing Exchanges*

Smith wrote often of the offerings made to him by elite Algonquians, boasting that he personally had "receaved contribution from 35 of their kings" (Smith et al. 1986, 1:176–177). His use of the word "contribution" emphasized the something-for-nothing form of these transactions. Smith's keen appreciation of gift economics often enabled him to accomplish the goals of the settlers by acquiring material goods at the lowest exchange price and appease Algonquian protocol by exhibiting the trust inherent to gift exchange. Smith also lured the Mamanatowick into making the indigenous exchange policy explicit by haggling with the Algonquian leader. When Smith asked for the native exchange value of a single English hatchet in January of 1608, an annoyed Chief Powhatan bristled at the request. He responded that the colonists should make something-for-nothing offers to him. Then, and only then, would they be compensated. Smith reported the details, noting that, "Not being agreed to trade for corne, hee [Chief Powhatan] desired to see all our Hatchets and Copper together, for which he would give us corne; with that auncient tricke the Chickahomaniens had oft acquainted me: his offer I refused, offering first to see what hee would give for one piece. He seeming to despise the nature of a Merchant, did scorne to sell, but *we freely should give him, and he liberally would requite us*" (Italics added; Smith et al. 1986, 1:71).

This historical passage included multiple gift-related insights that merit discussion. Powhatan declared that he did not *agree to trade* and that exchange with him consisted of mutual gifts. He mandated separate and reciprocal something-for-nothing offerings as opposed to an immediate something-for-something trade. Smith meanwhile demonstrated a European tendency to embrace commodity economics through his offer "first to see what hee would give for one piece." The passage is a clear example of the contrast between the distinct exchange systems.

In the process of demanding gift exchange from the English, Chief Powhatan also condemned the Chickahominies and their *merchant* practices. The Mamanatowick's instincts and insults are substantiated in the historical records, which affirmed that the Chickahominies were indeed economically distinct from the surrounding tribes. Embodying the definition of a merchant—a person who buys and sells goods for a profit—the Chickahominies engaged in commodity exchange. Except for instances when the English used violent means to coerce the natives, the Chickahominies never initiated gift giving with the colonists. According to existing historical records, the Chickahominies were the only Chesapeake tribe that repeatedly exchanged items with European colonists that were predominantly commodities. In fact, contemporary primary sources indicated that the Chickahominies and the English engaged in trade twice as often as gift exchange. This finding is especially distinct considering that gifts made up over three-quarters of the total transactions in this study (Mallios 1998).

## Exchange between Individuals of Similar Rank

Elite Algonquians repeatedly attempted to ensure that reciprocal gift exchange with the Europeans occurred between members of like status. The historical records offer multiple accounts of the natives closely monitoring the link between exchange and status. Three examples follow. The first emphasizes how the Algonquians equated high rank with a right to receive gifts. The second distinguishes different forms of exchange for Algonquians of different status. The third demonstrates how generosity and high status were intertwined in the Algonquian cosmology.

### EXAMPLE 1

When English leaders at Roanoke Island made offerings to Roanoacs who were socially inferior to the head weroance, Chief Granganimeo seized the goods. The Algonquian leader declared that, "all things ought to be deliuered" to him because "the rest were but his seruants, and followers" (Quinn 1955:100). Elite status entitled one to receive gifts. Barlowe noted, "when Granganimeo, the kings brother was present, none durst (to) trade but himselfe, except such as weare redde peeces of copper on their heads, like himselfe: for that is the difference betweene the Noble men, and Gouerners of Countries, and the meaner sort" (Quinn 1955:103). In gift economies like the Algonquian exchange system, status and exchange were closely interrelated, while in commodity economies an individual's rank was often entirely separate from the transaction.

### EXAMPLE 2

Smith noted the details of a conversation between Chief Powhatan and Englishman Captain Newport that included an important indigenous division between type of exchange and rank. It also further verified the Mamanatowick's customary practice of engaging in exchanges that took the form of something for nothing. Smith recorded that Chief Powhatan told Newport that, "It is not agreeable to my [Chief Powhatan's] greatnesse in this pedling manner to trade for trifles; and I esteeme you [Captain Newport] also a great Werowance. Therefore lay me down all your commodities together, what I like I will take, and in recompence give you that I thinke fitting their value" (Smith et al. 1986, 1:217).

Chief Powhatan established a bond not only between the two leaders—himself and Newport—but between elite Algonquians and the practice of gift exchange as well. He blended the verifications of his *greatnesse* and Newport's qualifications of high social ranking with the norms of gift exchange. Gifts and counter-gifts were *agreeable* forms of exchange for elite individuals according to Powhatan economic practices; trade was not.

Example 3

Smith also observed that "the great presents [that] Newport" gave to the Mamanatowick "confirmed [the natives'] opinion of [the Captain's] greatnesse" (Smith et al. 1986, 1:215). The natives explicitly linked social dominance and gift giving. Smith repeatedly noted that status and generosity were intertwined in the indigenous world. He stated that it was "wrought . . . into the Salvages understandings" a connection between Algonquian social standing and magnanimity (Smith et al. 1986, 1:215).

*Acquisition of Debt Versus Wealth*

In asserting that the Powhatans had "no respect for profitt," Jamestown colonist Gabriel Archer provided weighty evidence that Chesapeake Algonquians did not participate in a commodity economy (Barbour 1969, 1:101). In repeatedly failing to engineer exchanges that turned an immediate profit, the indigenous population demonstrated that the acquisition of wealth was not their objective. Whereas Archer's observation affirmed the impossibility of systematically labeling Powhatan transactions as commodities, Smith summarized the collective success of the indigenous gift exchange. He acknowledged the effectiveness of the Powhatan gift economy, commenting to the Mamanatowick that, "By the gifts you bestow on me, you gaine more then by trade" (Smith et al. 1986, 1:249). Smith admitted that Powhatan gifts had placed him in debt to the Mamanatowick and other weroances. The Algonquian leaders would likely accumulate more through the payment of debt—in return offerings—than they would have reaped through trade.

*Valuing the Bond over the Goods*

Traditional English market transactions occurred regardless of interpersonal amicability. Smith emphasized that, "you should know it is not our custome, to sell our curtesies as a vendible commodity" (Smith et al. 1986, 1:249). This statement reveals the contrast in relational requirements between gift and commodity economies. Whereas elite Algonquian gift exchange relied on friendly relations between transactors, English transactions occurred regardless of interpersonal amicability. Simply put, although indigenous cordiality was not for sale, it was an integral part of the native economic system. The exchange-partner bond was so important that Chief Powhatan refused to trade when he thought it had been compromised. Bringing weaponry to the trade table was particularly offensive, the presence of which signified a lack of trust. Chief Powhatan observed that the English rarely came to exchange "in [a] friendly manner"; they always brought "guns and swords, as [if] to invade . . . foes" (Smith et al. 1986, 1:248). Smith observed that the Mamanatowick "expected to have all these [English] men lay their armes at his feet" when trading (Smith et al. 1986, 1:265). In an attempt to reestablish trust by emphasizing interpersonal bonds over the utility of trade goods, Chief Powhatan declared that he would only guarantee transactions with the English if they exchanged without their weapons.

## Accusations of Gift-Exchange Violations

In early 1609, Chief Powhatan complained that Smith had failed to provide him with satisfactory return offerings. The Mamanatowick told the English leader that, "I never used any Werowance, so kindely as your selfe, yet from you I receive the least kindnesse of any. Captaine Newport gave me swords, copper, cloathes, a bed, tooles, or what I desired; ever taking what I offered him, and would send away his gunnes when I intreated him: none doth deny to lye at my feet or refuse to doe what I desire, but onely you; of whom I can have nothing but what you regard not, and yet you will have whatsoever you demand" (Smith et al. 1986, 1:248). Only an individual who expected reciprocation would likely lament not receiving it. In addition, each issue on the Mamanatowick's list of grievances focused on the relationship between himself and Smith. The reasons he was upset—Smith did not always accept what Powhatan offered, Smith refused to visit unarmed, and Smith did not always grant Powhatan's requests—all concerned appropriate behavior by gift-exchange partners. In his reprimand, the Mamanatowick never disputed the value of the goods involved in the transactions. To emphasize the personal nature of these socioeconomic injustices, Powhatan compared Smith's actions to Newport's behavior. How could these slights be cultural differences, the Algonquian leader implied, if Newport behaved so appropriately? The Mamanatowick pinpointed Smith's gift-exchange violations, contrasted them with Newport's more appropriate actions, and in doing so, he was revealing that their exchange-partner bond, as well as the intercultural accord, was in jeopardy.

## Non-Elite Exchange

Historical records revealed a division between Algonquian status and exchange type. Although gift exchange was reserved for transactions between the leaders of each group, low-status natives usually engaged the settlers in commodity exchange. Whereas over 80 percent of the transactions between English and Algonquian leaders were gifts, lower-ranking natives traded commodities with the colonists nearly two-thirds of the time. Smith noticed that low-status Algonquians often refused to trade with the settlers until they had first offered gifts to him. The commodity-based interaction began with the non-elite natives making initial tribute-like offerings to the English leader. These gifts flattered and obliged Smith, ensuring amicable trade between the colonists and Algonquians. Acquisition of English trade goods, facilitated by preliminary gift offerings, enabled many low-status natives to move up the Algonquian hierarchy without consent from the weroances or Mamanatowick. This would significantly transform relations over time, as it gravely altered Algonquian cultural norms and practices, likely disrupting the pervasive power and influence of Chief Powhatan and the other lesser weroances.

## Spanish Missionary Exchange Practices

The mission system fueled Spain's colonial undertakings in the Americas (Connolly 1967; Thomas 1990; Deagan 1990; Lyon 1976, 1990; Weber 1992; Codignola 1995; Oberg 1999). Like the commodity ventures of other colonial settlements, the mission system generated immediate wealth for Spain in the form of goods, land, and people. The missions transformed potentially antagonistic natives into a laboring class that served the colony and crown (Milanich 1999:xiv). The missionaries did so under the auspices of spiritual enlightenment. Using indigenous labor, missionaries built La Florida into a center of profit for the Spanish monarchy. In essence, missionization was colonialism; it endeavored to manipulate both the land and its native population (Milanich 1999:xiii). Across the different regions and particular religious sects, missions were a relatively cheap and effective way of creating an indigenous working class (Beaver 1988:435–439; Kan 1988; White 1991; Weber 1992; Brown 1992:26; McEwan 1993, 1995; Jackson and Castillo 1995:31–39; Milanich 1995; John 1996; Wagner 1998: 443; Axtell 2001; Taylor 2001; Lightfoot 2005:6).

Yet there was a spiritual and economic duality to this system. Many missionaries desired neither the accumulation of riches nor debt. Their primary goal was the conversion of non-Christians. They embraced exchanges that helped the cause and forbade transactions that obstructed it (Polzer 1976:39). The missionization process was often at odds with commercial endeavors (Hutchinson 1969; Guest 1978). Although no missionary guidebook explicitly directed the clerics in their endeavors, Jesuit ventures in North America followed a standardized sequence (Polzer 1976:39). Historian Charles Polzer described an evolutionary model for the missions of the Society of Jesus and detailed four phases. He wrote that, "These stages can be classified according to 1) a pre-mission phase (or *entrada*), 2) a mission phase (or *conversion*), 3) a doctrinal or preparochial phase (or *doctrina*), and 4) the secularization phase (or *parroquia*)" (Italics original; Polzer 1976:47).

During the pre-mission phase, Jesuits attempted to do little more than introduce themselves to the natives (Polzer 1976:48). Initial encounters provided opportunities for the clerics to offer religious goods to the indigenous population. The gifts always took the form of the most ornate objects of Catholic culture (Polzer 1976:47). Crucifixes, crosses, rosaries, and other items drew the natives close (Thomas 1988:117; Guest 1994:266; Lightfoot 2005:84). The offerings increased indigenous curiosity in Christianity and demonstrated the Jesuits' good will. All of these factors increased the Fathers' chances of successfully proselytizing natives. Eye-catching gifts with European religious significance lured indigenous inhabitants near and gave the Jesuits an opening to forge sacramental links with potential converts (Polzer 1976:48). The missionaries insisted on bringing the sacred items on their soul-saving ventures, even when the sacred items encumbered travel.

After repeatedly attempting to convince natives of the benefits of Catholicism, clerics waited for them to request baptism (Polzer 1976:41). Indigenous appeals for spiritual rebirth marked the end of the pre-mission phase. When the Jesuits baptized natives, they offered them an opportunity of eternal salvation through purification and forgiveness of past sins (Bangert 1972). The missionaries' gifts of baptism to the natives acted as immediate and long-term investments for the Church and Crown. Mission Indians made up the overwhelming majority of La Florida's manual labor (Milanich 1999:xii). Although the Jesuits at Ajacan were not successful in their soul-saving venture, many American missions prospered and evolved through all four of Polzer's stages. By the last phase, secularization, the Spanish Empire exacted payment from neophytes. The King of Spain granted a 10-year tax exemption to recently converted natives (Spicer 1962:292). Once the grace period elapsed, neophytes began to repay in part the missionaries' initial gift of baptism to them. In turning to Catholicism the natives maintained the clerical duty for the proselytization of others and acquired the burden of supporting the Crown.

Jesuits generally expected indigenous populations to provide food for them for as long as it took the clerics to find a way to sustain themselves. At Ajacan, what the missionaries lacked in food supplies and trade goods, they made up with religious items. Since the ornate and sacred goods of the Church frequently piqued the interest of the non-Christian and led to requests for baptism, Father Segura decided that these sacred items took precedence over food or trade supplies. When offering an opportunity of attaining salvation, the clerics took the native gifts of food for granted. As long as proselytization proved successful, the Jesuits were rarely preoccupied with obtaining their own sustenance.

The religious concerns of the mission system often conflicted with its colonial profiteering goals. The offer of an opportunity at salvation was ideally a pure gift. Acceptance of the missionary gift was faith, which also acted as reciprocation. The clerics were a conduit for the message of their god, and their goal was to spread the word. Since the missionaries often lived off of the charity of the indigenous population during the initial stages of the proselytizing process, this true gift became part of reciprocal gift exchange. Mutual something-for-nothing offerings passed between the two groups. Yet Spain built its colonial empires on immediate profit from the goods, labor, and organizing talents of the converts. This socioeconomic multiplicity led to strikingly different interpretations and strategies by members of the mission system.

When Father Segura toured failing missions in La Florida in the late 1560s, he developed a proselytizing philosophy that was extreme in terms of its views of trade and profit. Although Segura's policy was extreme, it should be noted that other clerics, when reflecting on the actual practice of missionization, grew disenfranchised with the results. For example, the California Fernandinos in the 1700s were infuriated with soldier and settler immorality and consequently disbanded the mission-pueblo program in the west (Lightfoot 2005:63). Segura and other clerics who shared his views found commodity exchanges to be detrimental to their goal of spiritually enlightening non-Christians. Segura saw the natives as pure and the Americas—the "New World"—as a paradise (Helms 1988:224–225; Merrell 1989). The Jesuits envisioned Ajacan as a second Eden with a beauty and bounty that pre-dated Original Sin (Mallios 2005b, 2007). Anthropologist Mary Helms and others have identified a common European perception regarding the alleged purity of America's indigenous population (Helms 1988; Todorov 1984; Axtell 1992; Kupperman 1995). Helms asserted that, "As a place of 'paradise existing,' the New World and its inhabitants represented a life prior to the Fall from Grace that was 'not yet' corrupt and 'still' in ideal harmony" (Helms 1988:224–225; Elliott 1970; Sheehan 1980). Roanoke colonist

Thomas Harriot included Theodore De Bry's portrait of *Adam and Eve in Eden* in a volume that contained artist John White's illustrations of the Carolina indigenous population and his own written descriptions of the 16th-century Algonquians (Harriot and White 1972). The natives were so pure in his mind that biblical innocence corresponded with any New-World indigenous human life. John S. C. Abbott, a 19th-century Congregationalist minister who authored many books on Spanish colonization of the Western hemisphere, echoed this sentiment, describing precontact native society as "before the fall" (Abbott 1873:159).

Missionary gifts of religious trinkets aided in the conversion process by raising native interest in their faith and demonstrating charity. On the contrary, bartering and attempts at maximizing material wealth disrupted proselytization. For a number of reasons clerics depended on native gifts of sustenance in order to survive. Their supplies frequently ran out prematurely. In addition, their unfamiliarity with the local terrain restricted their ability to obtain food. Commodity exchange disrupted the sequence of reciprocal gift giving that solidified interpersonal amicability. Furthermore, these Jesuits feared the self-interest and desire for personal gain that came with these trades. Ultimately, they worried that greed would contaminate the assumed purity of the natives.

Resulting from this desire to protect the natives from material corruption, the Chesapeake Jesuits prohibited trade with the Ajacan Algonquians. Father Segura gave one qualification on their mandate forbidding trade. He declared that Jesuit dealings with the natives had to be "in the way judged fitting here" (Lewis and Loomie 1953:92). Segura and the Jesuits pursued a singular goal at Ajacan, the conversion of Don Luis's tribe to Christianity. They prohibited any kind of interaction that interfered with the ultimate native spiritual transformation. Historians Clifford Lewis and Albert Loomie remarked that, "Clearly, he [Segura] wanted to teach the [Ajacan] Indians their duty of supporting the missionaries and also keep the natives from contamination from white traders and their wares" (Lewis and Loomie 1953:43).

Although strict rules governed the interaction between the missionaries and the natives they intended to proselytize, no such restrictions hampered exchanges between clerics and the natives they did not plan to convert. While maintaining a primary goal of non-Christian conversion, Segura employed a version of the missionary economy that included aspects of commodity exchange when engaging other neighboring indigenous inhabitants. In many instances of missionization, the clerics only aimed at initially converting a specific group. In the Chesapeake, the Jesuits focused on the Ajacan natives with former member Don Luis as their interpreter and intermediary. Segura and his cadre, however, maintained the option of trading with other nearby natives who did not belong to Don Luis's former tribe (Lewis and Loomie 1953:109). Part gift economy and part commodity economy, Segura's implementation of the missionary exchange system was essentially different from both exchange systems. The conversion of non-Christians took center stage, making the accumulation of debt or wealth entirely peripheral. Unbeknownst to him, this distinction would contribute to the mission's failure and to his own death.

## English Colonial Exchange Practices

A desire for profit was deeply imbedded in the minds of the English colonists at Roanoke and Jamestown (Kupperman 1995:1; Oberg 1999; cf. Mintz 1985; Wallerstein 1974, 1980, 1989). They tried to acquire immediate wealth in their transactions, prizing the European material value of the goods involved in the exchange. The members of a financial group known as the Virginia Company had been the primary investors in the Jamestown venture, and they expected to earn dividends. Consequently, the colonists were instructed to obtain vendible commodities from the Americas. They perceived the Western hemisphere as a plentiful source of valuable foreign materials that would free England from its dependence on dangerous privateering jaunts (Kupperman 1984:32). Accordingly, Roanoke's Thomas Harriot included a list of "Merchantable commodities" in his report of the Carolinas (Quinn 1955:325). John Smith's *Map of Virginia* . . . contained a similar inventory of "The Commodities in Virginia" (Smith et al. 1986, 1:159). Roanoke colonist Arthur Barlowe even provided the English value of trade goods in his relation, itemizing: "[a] tinne dishe for twentie skinnes, woorth twentie Crownes, . . . a copper kettle for fiftie skinnes woorth fiftie Crownes," and so forth. (Quinn 1955:101). Commodity lists and price indices allowed the benefactors of English colonialism to know the bottom line—profit. Embodying the capitalistic extreme of these ventures, Englishman George Peckham even advocated the establishment of a trinket industry based on the labor of idle English children to produce goods that would be traded for American commodities. In 1583 he wrote that, "children of 12 and 14 years of age or under, may be kept from idleness, in making a thousand kinds of trifling things, which will be good Merchandize for that Country [the Americas]" (Jehlen and Warner 1997:62). Elite English sought to exploit North America's indigenous population in ways similar to how they were already exploiting English commoners (Kupperman 1980).

Unlike the Algonquians, English colonists expressed little concern for social rank when exchanging with the indigenous population. Of primary importance was the material value of the items transacted. For example, Roanoke Governor Ralph Lane was indiscriminate about who his trading partners were as he attempted to exchange copper for Ossomocomuck food, expressing it could be "any of them" (Quinn 1955:266). In dealings with the Carolina natives, Lane prized access to exotic goods over any interpersonal bonds between himself and any Algonquian, elite or otherwise. In addition, Jamestown leaders frequently initiated trade with low-ranking natives, requiring only that the exchange resulted in food for the settlement.

Profit through trade was not only the preeminent goal of those who planned the Jamestown venture; it was also thought to be a way to ensure amicable intercultural relations. Jamestown's London directors had complete faith in the ability of equitable trade to satisfy parties of both cultures (Quitt 1995:229). English officials prided themselves on the voluntary nature of free trade and contrasted their policies with Spanish colonizers whose spiritual and economic aims were forced on indigenous peoples (Fausz 1977:157). Budding capitalists saw free trade as natural and a perfect fit for the unspoiled native people and indigenous markets of North America.

Concerns regarding commodity-economy transgressions repeatedly surfaced in the historical texts surrounding English colonization of Jamestown Island. On multiple occasions, Smith lamented in his narratives how new colonists to the area routinely flooded indigenous areas with European exchange goods and thus devalued the settlement's only means of obtaining food. This commodity-exchange transgression was of little concern to the mariners who spent much of their time sailing the Atlantic and trading with indigenous peoples at various ports. Smith and his colleagues suffered the consequences of these shortsighted economic violations. In 1606, the London Council warned potential Chesapeake colonists of the dangers of inundating native society with European trade goods. Their official "Instructions given by way of advice" reminded the impending settlers that, "You must take Care that your Marriners that Go for wages Do not marr your trade [with the Powhatans] for those that mind not to inhabit for a Little Gain will Debase the Estimation of Exchange and hinder the trade for Ever after" (Barbour 1969, 1:53). The instructions went largely unheeded, foreshadowing later exchange-based troubles between the English and Algonquians.

## Overall Exchange Pattern

Middle Atlantic Algonquians dealt with European transgressions of indigenous gift economies in ways that were consistent with native political, economic, and social systems. Different socioeconomic affronts by colonists warranted distinct Algonquian punishments. There were seven types of European exchange transgressions:

(1) failure to give,
(2) failure to accept,
(3) failure to reciprocate,
(4) exchange with tribute rivals after failing to give, accept, or reciprocate,
(5) economic inundation,
(6) hostility toward a gift-exchange partner, and
(7) permanent removal of an elite gift-exchange partner.

The Algonquians met these economic offenses with four distinct reactions:

(1) no response,
(2) desertion,
(3) indirect or delayed violence, and
(4) direct violence.

A map of exchange violations and indigenous responses demonstrated that native behavior occurred in a strikingly consistent pattern (Table 6.1).

Links between socioeconomic crimes and punishments centered on the interpersonal bonds established between exchange partners through gift giving. In reaction to economic violations that merely strained the bonds, natives responded with nonviolent punishments. Failures to give, accept, and reciprocate, as well as individual hostile acts toward gift-exchange partners resulted in desertion or diminished interaction. These transgressions alienated individuals previously bonded by gifts, driving them apart both literally and figuratively. When faced with European refusals to reciprocate, Ajacan Algonquians, Roanoacs, and Paspaheghs each chose first to abandon the colonists rather than assault them. Additional European socioeconomic offenses that followed the native alienation then contributed to indigenous hostilities.

Algonquian groups met a certain kind of European exchange-system transgression with delayed violence. Specifically, these types of violations were transgressions that continually eroded a link that was once established by gift offerings. Flooding native society with Western goods devalued the trade items and the European presence in the Americas for the Algonquians. The natives shifted their emphasis in exchange from the link between people to the individually transacted goods. Inundation debased English trade goods, strangled

Table 6.1. Exchange violations and consequences

| Date | Locale | Economic violations | Consequences |
|------|--------|---------------------|--------------|
| 8/1570 | Ajacan | Failure to reciprocate | Desertion |
| 1/1571 | Ajacan | Exchange with tribute rivals after failure to reciprocate | Direct violence |
| 12/1585 | Roanoke | Hostility toward gift-exchange partner | Indirect violence |
| 12/1585 | Roanoke | Permanent removal of an elite gift-exchange partner (Granganimeo) | Indirect violence |
| 3/1586 | Roanoke | Failure to reciprocate | No response |
| 4/1586 | Roanoke | Failure to accept | No response |
| 4/1586 | Roanoke | Failure to reciprocate | Desertion |
| 4/1586 | Roanoke | Permanent removal of an elite gift-exchange partner (Ensenore) | Direct violence |
| 6/1586 | Roanoke | Hostility toward gift-exchange partner (friendly fire) | No response |
| 8/1587 | Roanoke | Hostility toward gift-exchange partner (friendly fire) | No response |
| 5/1607 | Jamestown | Failure to reciprocate | Desertion |
| 5/1607 | Jamestown | Exchange with tribute rivals after failure to reciprocate | Direct violence |
| 10/1607 | Jamestown | Market inundation | Delayed violence |
| 1/1608 | Jamestown | Market inundation | Delayed violence |
| 3/1608 | Jamestown | Failure to accept | Indirect violence |
| 6–8/1608 | Jamestown | Exchange with tribute rivals after failure to reciprocate | Direct violence |
| 10/1608 | Jamestown | Market inundation | Delayed violence |
| 1/1609 | Jamestown | Failure to give | Direct violence |
| 1/1609 | Jamestown | Failure to reciprocate | Direct violence |
| 10/1609 | Jamestown | Hostility toward gift-exchange partner | Direct violence |
| 10/1609 | Jamestown | Failure to reciprocate | Direct violence |
| 10/1609 | Jamestown | Permanent removal of an elite gift-exchange partner (Smith) | Direct violence |

exchange, and led to eventual hostilities. The repeated European exchange glut gradually deteriorated intercultural relations. It initially transformed the natives and Europeans from gift-giving allies to commodity-trading aliens, and then ultimately to hostile enemies.

At Ajacan, Roanoke, and Jamestown, the indigenous population countered European economic violations that entirely eliminated the gift-based interpersonal bonds with immediate violence. In exchanging with the social rivals of an Algonquian group that had just been shunned, the Europeans humiliated the natives. This form of social embarrassment demanded immediate retribution. The permanent removal of an elite exchange partner also severed the gift-based bond. With the emphasis in gift exchange on the individuals and their bond as opposed to the transacted goods, the death or departure of an exchange partner left no link between the two groups. In addition, any combination of multiple economic transgressions resulted in prompt hostilities.

Algonquians frequently offered false gifts to European groups before avenging their gift-based socioeconomic slights with violence. On several occasions the natives made duplicitous something-for-nothing gestures to colonists who had violated the indigenous gift economy. Don Luis presented grain to Quiros and his men and then killed them. The former neophyte also offered labor to Segura before murdering the remaining Jesuits at Ajacan. The Mamanatowick repeatedly gave food, labor, and prestigious goods to Smith and his crew moments before attempting to annihilate them. Opechancanough also preceded an intended assault on the English with a set of false gifts. The natives lured the settlers into their ambushes with false offerings because the deception and the violence effectively punished the Europeans for their past economic transgressions and symbolically showcased the colonists' exchange-system violations. The duplicity and hostility reaffirmed Algonquian cultural rules of exchange and justice and demonstrated the consequences of disregarding these standards.

Don Luis's two attacks on the Jesuits were not lone instances of lethal and symbolic assaults. Native groups across North America repeatedly led similar types of raids on European settlers. In Virginia during the winter of 1609–10, starving Jamestown colonists stole food from neighboring Algonquians only to be found later "slain, with their mouths stopped full of bread" (Percy 1967:265). There are also historical accounts of 18th-century natives from the Great Lakes region filling the mouths of their European casualties with dirt, symbolizing the colonists' lust for indigenous lands (Gleach 1997:51). These episodes of symbolic violence coincided with the goals of Algonquian warfare that, although devastatingly lethal, were corrective, restorative, and instructive for fellow natives (Gleach 1997:51). Don Luis's attacks met these objectives. By providing the natives with the Jesuits' goods that they were owed, the assaults and consequent looting righted a wrong and corrected an improper inaction. In the case of Don Luis and Father Segura, the hostility restored justice by punishing the clerics who had denied the alliance and socially humiliated the Ajacan natives. It is also probable that the identity of the final false gift that Don Luis offered to Segura—the erection of a church—was highly symbolic. It likely mocked how the missionaries' primary purpose was entirely reliant on the indigenous population. In addition, the violence taught proper behavior by demonstrating the rules of the indigenous gift-exchange system and the consequences of violating these obligations. Don Luis's poetically just hostilities were lessons that emphasized the essence and practice of the Algonquian gift economy.

There are two exceptions to this pattern of European economic transgressions and indigenous punishments. When the Algonquians believed that a colonist had acquired the ability to revive themselves or others, they ignored the exchange-system violations of the settler's comrades. The Roanoacs followed Lane's seemingly supernatural return from certain doom at the hands of the mighty Chawanoacs with offerings of peace. Likewise, Smith's apparent resuscitation of the asphyxiated Chickahominy youth also warded off impending hostility and yielded multiple gifts. The display or rumor of an individual European's seemingly otherworldly power resulted in immediate indigenous pardons for past socioeconomic affronts by the colonists. The second exception to native punishment for European exchange-system transgressions occurred when an intercultural alliance served to better an Algonquian tribe's positioning within the native social hierarchy. The Chawanoacs and Croatoans both chose to look past the same types of English gift-exchange offenses that had inspired other tribes to strike when it resulted in greater political gains.

The events at Ajacan, Roanoke, and Jamestown showcased the rules of native gift economies in different ways. Interaction at Ajacan demonstrated straightforward European violations and resultant Algonquian punishments. The details of early attempted English settlement at Roanoke provided exceptions to expected economic norms; the natives overlooked exchange offenses and their usual penalties for bigger sociopolitical goals. The inaugural years of England's Jamestown colony included extensively intertwined gift- and commodity-exchange transgressions that led to conflict. The direct example (Ajacan), the exceptional example (Roanoke), and the convoluted example (Jamestown) all detailed cultural clashes and emphasized a link between failed gifts and bloodshed.

In all three case studies, the exchanges followed a general pattern. Although the events at Ajacan, Roanoke, and Jamestown differed significantly from one another, the overall trend was

Gift exchange → Economic violation → Commodity exchange → Economic violation → Violence . . .

Within each distinct colonization attempt, early interaction between colonists and indigenous peoples consisted mostly of gift exchanges, middle contact included a majority of commodity exchanges, and late interaction was almost entirely violent. Exchange-system violations undermined the bonds established by initial gift giving and alienated the Europeans and Algonquians. The groups frequently continued to interact and exchange commodities, but further economic transgressions worsened relations and led to hostilities. Native attacks resulted in either the elimination of the colonists or the offering of gifts to secure peace. These presents that ensured the cease-fire started the "G→EV→C→EV→V . . . " sequence once again. Although the pattern refers to three closely interrelated settlements, this model may be applicable cross-culturally, especially in contact contexts (White 1991:400–404; Lightfoot 2005:235). This model resembles Martin Quitt's stages, but is cyclical instead of linear (Quitt 1995:244; Oberg 1999:6).

The individual identity of different indigenous tribes played a crucial role at each historic locale. The Ajacan natives and their neighbors competed against each other in a burgeoning tributary system. Likewise, the individual Carolina tribes actively antagonized one another and frequently shifted alliances in a continuing power struggle. Furthermore, Chief Powhatan ruled over 30 different groups of Chesapeake Algonquians, each distinct, especially in terms of their interaction with Europeans. For example, the Nansamunds repeatedly initiated attacks against the Jamestown colonists regardless of overall English/Powhatan relations. The Chickahominies, in addition to being politically independent, demonstrated their economic distinctiveness as well by transacting commodities with the European settlers instead of gifts. Overall, the nuances of relations between tribes significantly altered intercultural alliances.

Rigorous application of Mauss's gift-exchange model to the detail-rich historical records regarding events at Ajacan, Roanoke, and Jamestown offered an additional explanation as to why Middle Atlantic Algonquians annihilated some European colonists and allowed others to survive. The cultural clash of distinctly different exchange systems frequently contributed to highly lethal, symbolic, and self-affirming Algonquian aggression against the Europeans. Mauss's belief that gifts act as a social contract between individuals, one that ensures peace and prevents violence, has a negative counterpart. As was seen repeatedly in the contact-period Chesapeake and Carolinas, failed gift exchange often causes hostilities. Gift giving never leaves the parties involved and their relationship unchanged. It either brings people closer together, securing their alliance, or pushes them apart toward hostilities. Although individuals who violate the economic norms of gift exchange may intend no deliberate malice, severe consequences often follow. Beware the gift and revere the gift, for it is simultaneously the offer of alliance and the mandate of reciprocity.

# References

Abbott, John S. C.
 1873    Ferdinand de Soto: The Discoverer of the Mississippi. New York: Dodd and Mead.
Althusser, Louis, and Étienne Balibar
 1968    Reading *Capital*. Ben Brewster, trans. London: Verso.
Appadurai, Arjun
 1986    Introduction: Commodities and the Politics of Value. *In* The Social Life of Things: Commodities in Cultural Perspective. Arjun Appadurai, ed. Pp. 3–63. Cambridge: Cambridge University Press.
Armitage, David
 1995    From Richard Hakluyt to William Robertson. *In* America in European Consciousness, 1493–1750. Karen Ordahl Kupperman, ed. Pp. 52–78. Chapel Hill: Published for the Institute of Early American History and Culture, Williamsburg, Va. by the University of North Carolina Press.
Axtell, James
 1981    The European and the Indian: Essays in the Ethnohistory of Colonial North America. New York: Oxford University Press.
 1985    The Invasion Within: The Contest of Cultures in Colonial North America. New York: Oxford University Press.
 1988    After Columbus: Essays in the Ethnohistory of Colonial North America. New York: Oxford University Press.
 1992    Beyond 1492: Encounters in Colonial North America. New York: Oxford University Press.
 2001    Natives and Newcomers: The Cultural Origins of North America. New York: Oxford University Press.
Bangert, William V.
 1972    A History of the Society of Jesus. St. Louis: Institute of Jesuit Sources.
Bannon, John Francis
 1967    The Spanish Borderlands Frontier, 1513–1821. New York: Holt Rinehart and Winston.

Barbour, Philip

1964    The Three Worlds of Captain John Smith. Boston: Houghton Mifflin.

1970    Pocahontas and Her World. Boston: Houghton Mifflin.

Barbour, Philip, ed.

1969    The Jamestown Voyages under the First Charter, 1606–1609: Documents Relating to the Foundation of Jamestown and the History of the Jamestown Colony up to the Departure of Captain John Smith, Last President of the Council in Virginia under the First Charter, Early in October 1609. 2 Vols. London: published for the Hakluyt Society by Cambridge University Press.

Barcia, Andres

1951    Barcia's Chronological History of the Continent of Florida. Gainesville: University Press of Florida.

Beaver, R. P.

1988    Protestant Churches and the Indians. *In* Handbook of North American Indians, vol. 4: History of Indian-White Relations. W. E. Washburn, vol. ed. Washington, DC: Smithsonian Institution.

Bellamy, Edward

2003    Looking Backward. New York: Broadview Press.

Binford, Lewis

1964    Archaeological and Ethnohistorical Investigations of Cultural Diversity and Progressive Development among Aboriginal Cultures of Coastal Virginia and North Carolina. Ph.D. dissertation, Department of Anthropology, University of Michigan.

Blanton, Dennis

2000    Drought as a Factor in the Jamestown Colony. Historical Archaeology 34(4):74–81.

2004    The Climate Factor in Late Prehistoric and Post-Contact Human Affairs. *In* Indian and European Contact in Context: The Mid-Atlantic Region. Dennis B. Blanton and Julia A. King, eds. Pp. 6–21. Gainesville: University Press of Florida.

Bloch, M., and J. Parry

1989    Introduction: Money and the Morality of Exchange. *In* Money and the Morality of Exchange. M. Bloch and J. Parry, eds. Pp. 1–32. Cambridge: Cambridge University Press.

Borofsky, Robert

1997    Cook, Lono, Obeyesekere, and Sahlins. Current Anthropology 38(2):255–282.

Bourdieu, Pierre

1977a   Outline of a Theory of Practice. Cambridge: Cambridge University Press.

1997b   *Selections from* The Logic of Practice. *In* The Logic of the Gift: Toward an Ethic of Generosity. Alan Schrift, e d. Pp. 190–230. New York: Routledge.

1997c   *Marginalia—Some Additional Notes on* The Gift. *In* The Logic of the Gift: Toward an Ethic of Generosity. Alan Schrift, ed. Pp. 231–244. New York: Routledge.

Bradley, James W.

1977    The Pompey Center Site: The Impact of European Trade Goods, 1600–1620. Archaeological Society of New York, William M. Beauchamp Chapter Bulletin 2(1):1–19.

Brooks, James
    2002    Captives and Cousins: Slavery, Kinship, and Community in the Southwest Borderlands. Chapel Hill: University of North Carolina Press.

Brown, I. W.
    1992    Certain Aspects of French-Indian Interaction in Lower Louisiana. *In* Calumet and Fleur-De-Lys: Archaeology of Indian and French Contact in the Midcontinent. J. A. Walthall and T. E. Emerson, eds. Pp. 17–34. Washington, DC: Smithsonian Institution.

Busbecq, Ogier Ghislain de
    1694    The Four Epistles of A. G. Busbequius Concerning His Embassy into Turkey: Being Remarks upon Their Religion, Customs, Riches, Strength and Government of That People. . . . London: J. Taylor and J. Wyat.

Bushnell, Amy Turner
    1981    The King's Coffer: Proprietors of the Spanish Florida Treasury, 1565–1702. Gainesville: University Press of Florida.
    1990    The Sacramental Imperative: Catholic Ritual and Indian Sedentism in the Provinces of Florida. *In* Columbian Consequences, vol. 2: Archaeological and Historical Perspectives on the Spanish Borderlands East. D. H. Thomas, ed. Pp. 475–490. Washington, DC: Smithsonian Institution.

Carneiro, Robert L.
    1978    Political Expansion as an Expression of the Principle of Competitive Exclusion. *In* Origins of the State: The Anthropology of Political Evolution. R. Cohen and E. R. Service, eds. Pp. 205–223. Philadelphia: Institute for the Study of Human Issues.

Carrier, James G.
    1990    Gifts in a World of Commodities. Social Analysis 29:19–37.

Cheal, David
    1988    The Gift Economy. London: Routledge.

Clifford, James
    1988    The Predicament of Culture. Cambridge, MA: Harvard University Press.

Codignola, Luca
    1995    The Holy See and the Conversion of the Indians in French and British North America, 1486–1760. *In* America in European Consciousness 1493–1750. Karen Ordahl Kupperman, ed. Pp. 195–242. Chapel Hill: University of North Carolina Press.

Connolly, Matthew
    1967    The Missions of Florida. *In* Explorations and Settlements in the Spanish Borderlands: Their Religious Motivations. Michael Gannon, ed. Pp. 211–234. St. Augustine: Mission Nombre de Dios.

Connor, Jeanette Thurber
    1925    Colonial Records of Spanish Florida, 1570–80. 2 Vols. Fayetteville: Florida State Historical Society, Pub. No. 5.

128 / REFERENCES

Damon, Frederick

1980    The Kula and Generalized Exchange: Considering Some Unconsidered Aspects of the Elementary Structures of Kinship. Man 15(2):267–292.

1990    From Muyuw to the Trobriands: Transformations along the Northern Side of the Kula Ring. Tucson: University of Arizona Press.

1993    Representation and Experience in Kula and Western Exchange Spheres (Or, Billy). Research in Economic Anthropology 14:235–254.

Davis, Thomas W., and Kathleen M. Child

2000    Late Woodland Ceramics on the Coastal Plain: A Possible New Type from Carteret County, North Carolina. North Carolina Archaeology 78–92.

Deagan, Kathleen

1987    Artifacts of the Spanish Colonies of Florida and the Caribbean, 1500–1800. Washington, DC: Smithsonian Institution.

1990    Accommodation and Resistance: The Process and Impact of Spanish colonization in the Southeast. In Columbian Consequences, vol. 2: Archaeological and Historical Perspectives on the Spanish Borderlands East. D. H. Thomas, ed. Pp. 297–314. Washington, DC: Smithsonian Institution.

De Boer, Warren R.

1998    Subterranean Storage and Organization of Surplus: The View from Eastern North America. Southeastern Archaeology 7(1):1–20.

Dening, Greg

1980    Islands and Beaches: Discourse on a Silent Land, Marquesas, 1774–1880. Honolulu: University Press of Hawai'i.

Dennis, Matthew

1993    Cultivating a Landscape of Peace. Ithaca, NY: Cornell University Press.

Dent, Richard J., Jr.

1995    Chesapeake Prehistory: Old Traditions, New Directions. New York: Plenum.

Durkheim, Émile

1938    The Rules of Sociological Method. Chicago: Free Press.

Dye, David H.

1990    Warfare in the Sixteenth-Century Southeast: The de Soto Expedition in the Interior. In Columbian Consequences, vol. 2: Archaeological and Historical Perspectives on the Spanish Borderlands East. D. H. Thomas, ed. Pp. 211–222. Washington, DC: Smithsonian Institution.

Earle, Timothy

1978    Chiefdoms in Archaeological and Ethnohistorical Perspectives. Annual Review of Anthropology 16:279–308.

1991    The Evolution of Chiefdoms. In Chiefdoms: Power, Economy, and Ideology. Timothy Earle, ed. Pp. 1–15. Cambridge: Cambridge University Press.

1997    How Chiefs Come to Power: The Political Economy in Prehistory. Stanford, CA: Stanford University Press.

Elliott, J. H.

1970    The Old World and the New, 1492–1650. Cambridge: Cambridge University Press.

Emerson, Ralph Waldo
1997     Gifts. *In* The Logic of the Gift: Toward an Ethic of Generosity. Alan Schrift, ed. Pp. 25–27. New York: Routledge.

Ewen, Charles R.
1990     Soldier of Fortune: Hernando de Soto in the Territory of the Apalachee, 1539–1540. *In* Columbian Consequences, vol. 2: Archaeological and Historical Perspectives on the Spanish Borderlands East. D. H. Thomas, ed. Pp 83–91. Washington, DC: Smithsonian Institution.

Fairbanks, Charles H.
1968     Early Spanish Colonial Beads. The Conference on Historic Site Archaeology Papers (2)3–21, Institute of Archaeology and Anthropology, University of South Carolina, Columbia.

Fausz, J. Frederick
1977     The Powhatan Uprising of 1622: A Historical Study of Ethnocentrism and Cultural Conflict. Ph.D. dissertation, Department of History, College of William and Mary, Williamsburg, Virginia.

1981     Opechancanough: Indian Resistance Leader. *In* Struggle and Survival in Colonial America. David G. Sweet and Gary B. Nash, eds. Pp. 21– 37. Berkeley: University of California Press.

1984     Anglo-Indian Relations in Colonial North America. *In* Scholars and the Indian Experience: Critical Review of Recent Writing in the Social Sciences. W. R. Swagerty, ed. Pp. 33–50. Bloomington: Indiana University Press.

1985     Patterns of Anglo-Indian Aggression and Accommodation along the Mid-Atlantic Coast, 1584–1634. *In* Cultures in Contact: The European Impact of Native Institutions in Eastern North America, A.D. 1000–1800. William Fitzhugh, ed. Pp. 225–268. Washington, DC: Smithsonian Institution.

1987     The Invasion of Virginia: Indians, Colonization and the Conquest of Cant. Virginia Magazine of History and Biography 95(1):153–156.

1988     Merging and Emerging Worlds: Anglo-Indian Interest Groups and the Development of the Seventeenth-Century Chesapeake. *In* Colonial Chesapeake Society. Lois Green Carr, Philip D. Morgan, and Jean B. Russo, ed. Pp. 47–98. Chapel Hill: University of North Carolina Press.

1990     "An Abundance of Blood Shed on Both Sides": England's First Indian War, 1609–1614. Virginia Magazine of History and Biography 98:3–56.

1997     *Review of* Gleach, Powhatan's World and Colonial Virginia: A Conflict of Cultures. Virginia Magazine of History and Biography 105(4).

Feest, Christian F.
1966     Powhatan: A Study in Political Organisation. Wiener Volkerkundliche Mitteilungen 13:69–83.

1978     Virginia Algonquians. *In* Handbook of North American Indians, vol. 15: Northeast. Bruce G. Trigger, vol. ed. Pp. 253–270. Washington, DC: Smithsonian Institution.

Feest, Christian F., ed.

1987    Indians and Europe: An Interdisciplinary Collection of Essays. Aachen, Germany: Edition Herodot.

Fernández-Armesto, Felipe

1991    Columbus. Oxford: Oxford University Press.

Fitzgerald, William R., Dean H. Knight, and Allison Bain

1995    Untanglers of Matters Temporal and Cultural: Glass Beads and the Early Contact Period Huron Ball Site. Canadian Journal of Archaeology 19:117–138.

Fitzhugh, William W.

1985    Commentary on Part III. In Cultures in Contact: The European Impact on Native Cultural Institutions in Eastern North America, A.D. 1000–1800. William Fitzhugh, ed. Pp. 187–192. Washington, DC: Smithsonian Institution.

Flannery, Kent

1972    The Origins of the Village as a Settlement Type in Mesoamerica and the Near East: A Comparative Study. In Man, Settlement, and Urbanism. P. Ucko, ed. Pp. 23–53. London: Duckworth.

Font, P.

1931    Font's Complete Diary: The Chronicle of the Founding of San Francisco. Herbert Eugene Bolton, ed. Berkeley: University of California Press.

Francis, Peter, Jr.

1988    Glass Trade Beads of Europe. Lake Placid, NY: Lapis Route Books, Center for Bead Research.

Gallivan, Martin

2003    James River Chiefdoms: The Rise of Social Inequality in the Chesapeake. Lincoln: University of Nebraska Press.

2004    Reconnecting the Contact Period and Late Prehistory: Household and Community Dynamics in the James River Basin. In Indian and European Contact in Context: The Mid-Atlantic Region. Dennis B. Blanton and Julia A. King, eds. Pp. 22–46. Gainesville: University Press of Florida.

Geertz, Clifford

1995    Culture War. New York Review of Books:4–6.

Gell, Alfred

1992    Inter-Tribal Commodity Barter and Reproductive Gift-Exchange in Old Melanesia. In Barter, Exchange and Value: An Anthropological Approach. Caroline Humphrey and Stephen Hughes-Jones, eds. Pp. 142–168. Cambridge: Cambridge University Press.

Giddens, Anthony

1979    Central Problems in Social Theory: Action, Structure and Contradiction in Social analysis. London: Macmillan.

Gleach, Frederic W.

1996    Controlled Speculation: Interpreting the Saga of Pocahontas and John Smith.

*In* Reading Beyond Words: Contexts for Native History. Jennifer S. Brown and Elizabeth Vibert, eds. Pp. 5–18. Peterborough, ON: Broadview Press.

1997    Powhatan's World and Colonial Virginia: A Conflict of Cultures. Lincoln: University of Nebraska Press.

Godelier, Maurice

1996    The Enigma of the Gift. Chicago: University of Chicago Press.

2002    Some Things You Give. *In* The Enigma of Gift and Sacrifice. Edith Wyschogrod, Jean-Joseph Goux, and Eric Boynton, eds. Pp. 19–37. New York: Fordham University Press.

Gradie, Charlotte M.

1988    Spanish Jesuits in Virginia: The Mission That Failed. Virginia Magazine of History and Biography 96(2):131–56.

1990    Jesuit Missions in Spanish North America, 1566–1623. Ph.D. dissertation, Department of History, University of Connecticut-Storrs.

1993    The Powhatans in the Context of the Spanish Empire. *In* Powhatan Foreign Relations, 1500–1722. Helen Rountree, ed. Pp. 154–172. Charlottesville: University of Virginia Press.

Gregory, Chris

1982    Gifts and Commodities. London: Academic Press.

Guest, F. F.

1978    Mission Colonization and Political Control in Spanish California. Journal of San Diego History 24:97–116.

1994    The California Missions Were Far from Faultless. Southern California Quarterly 76(3):255–307.

Gutiérrez, Ramón A.

1991    When Jesus Came, the Corn Mothers Went Away: Marriage, Sexuality, and Power in New Mexico, 1500–1846. Stanford, CA: Stanford University Press.

Hallowell, A. Irving

1976    Contributions to Anthropology: Selected Papers of A. Irving Hallowell. Chicago: University of Chicago Press.

Hantman, Jeffrey L.

1990    Between Powhatan and Quirank: Reconstructing Monacan Culture and History in the Context of Jamestown. American Anthropologist 92(3):676–690.

1993    Powhatan's Relations with the Piedmont Monacans. *In* Powhatan Foreign Relations, 1500–1722. Helen Rountree, ed. Pp. 94–111. Charlottesville: University of Virginia Press.

Harriot, Thomas, and John White

1972    A Briefe and True Report of the New Found Land of Virginia. New York: Dover.

Harris, Elizabeth

1982    Nueva Cadiz and Associated Beads: A New Look. Archaeological Research Booklets 17, Lancaster, PA.

Hatfield, April

2003    Spanish Colonization Literature, Powhatan Geographies, and English Perceptions of Tsenacommacah/Virginia. Journal of Southern History 69(2):245–283.

Headley, John M.

1995    Campanella, America, and World Evangelization. In America in European Consciousness 1493–1750. Karen Ordahl Kupperman, ed. Pp. 243–271. Chapel Hill: University of North Carolina Press.

Healey, C.

1986    New Guinea Inland Trade. Special issue on recent studies in the political economy of PNG societies. Modjeska and D. Gardiner, eds. Pp. 146–163. Mankind 15.

Helms, Mary W.

1988    Ulysses' Sail: An Ethnographic Odyssey of Power, Knowledge, and Geographical Distance. Princeton, NJ: Princeton University Press.

Herbert, Joseph M.

1999    Prehistoric Pottery: Series and Sequence on the Carolina Coast. North Carolina Archaeology 48:1–106.

Hodges, Mary Ellen N.

1993    The Archaeology of Native American Life in Virginia in the Context of European Contact: Review of Past Research. In The Archaeology of 17th-Century Virginia. Theodore Reinhart, and Dennis Pogue, eds. Pp. 1–66. Richmond, VA: Dietz Press.

Hoffman, Paul

1980    The Spanish Crown and the Defense of the Caribbean. Baton Rouge: Louisiana State University Press.

1986    New Light on Vicente Gonzales's 1585 Voyage in Search of Raleigh's English Colonies. North Carolina Historical Review 63:199–223.

1990    A New Andalucia and a Way to the Orient: The American Southeast during the Sixteenth Century. Baton Rouge: Louisiana State University Press.

Holterman, J.

1970a    The Revolt of Estanislao. Wassaja, the Indian Historian 3(1):43–54.

1970b    The Revolt of Yozcolo: Indian Warrior in the Fight for Freedom. Wassaja, the Indian Historian 3(2):19–23.

Hoover, R. L.

1989    Spanish-Native Interaction and Acculturation in the Alta California Missions. In Columbian Consequences, vol. 1: Archaeological and Historical Perspectives on the Spanish Borderlands West. D. H. Thomas, ed. Pp. 396–506. Washington, DC: Smithsonian Institution.

Hudgins, Carter C.

2004    Old World Industries and New World Hope: The Industrial Role of Copper at Jamestown. Journal of the Jamestown Rediscovery Center 2.

Hudson, Charles, and Carmen Tesser, eds.

1994    The Forgotten Centuries: Indians and Europeans in the American South, 1521–1704. Athens: University of Georgia Press.

Hudson, Charles M., John E. Worth, and Chester B. DePratter
  1990    Refinements in Hernando de Soto's Route through Georgia and South Carolina.
          *In* Columbian Consequences, vol. 2: Archaeological and Historical Perspectives
          on the Spanish Borderlands East. D. H. Thomas, ed. Pp. 107–120. Washington, DC:
          Smithsonian Institution.

Huey, Paul R.
  1983    Glass Trade Beads from Fort Orange (1624–1676), Albany, New York. Proceedings
          of the 1982 Glass Bead Conference. Charles Hayes, ed. Pp. 83–110. Research Re-
          cords 16. Rochester: Rochester Museum and Science Division.

Hutchinson, C. A.
  1969    Frontier Settlement in Mexican California: The Hijar-Padres Colony and Its Ori-
          gins, 1769–1835. New Haven, CT: Yale University Press.

Hyde, Lewis
  1983    The Gift. London: Vintage.

Ignatius of Loyola
  1951    The Spiritual Exercises of St. Ignatius: Based on Studies in the Language of the
          Autograph. Louis J. Puhl, trans. Chicago: Loyola University Press.
  1959    Letters of St. Ignatius of Loyola. William J. Young, trans. Chicago: Loyola Univer-
          sity Press.

Irigaray, Luce
  1997    Women on the Market. *In* The Logic of the Gift: Toward an Ethic of Generosity.
          Alan Schrift, ed. Pp. 174–189. New York: Routledge.

Jackson, R. H., and E. Castillo
  1995    Indians, Franciscans, and Spanish Colonization: The Impact of the Mission Sys-
          tem on California Indians. Albuquerque: University of New Mexico Press.

Jehlen, Myra, and Michael Warner
  1997    The English Literatures of America, 1500–1800. New York: Routledge.

Jennings, Francis
  1975    The Invasion of America: Indians, Colonialism, and the Cant of Conquest. Chapel
          Hill: Published for the Institute of Early American History and Culture by the
          University of North Carolina Press.

John, E. A. H.
  1996    Storms Brewed in Other Men's Worlds: The Confrontation of Indians, Spanish,
          and French in the Southwest, 1540–1795. 2nd ed. Norman: University of Okla-
          homa Press.

Kan, S.
  1988    The Russian Orthodox Church in Alaska. *In* Handbook of North American Indi-
          ans, vol. 4: History of Indian-White Relations. W. E. Washburn, vol. ed. Pp. 506–
          521. Washington, DC: Smithsonian Institution.

Karklins, Karlis
  1974    Seventeenth Century Dutch Beads. Historical Archaeology 8:64–82.
  1985    Guide to the Description and Classification of Glass Beads. *In* Glass Beads. 2nd
          ed., Studies in Archaeology, Architecture, and History. Ottawa, ON: Parks Canada.

Kenyon, Ian T. and William R. Fitzgerald
  1986    Dutch Glass Beads in the Northeast: An Ontario Perspective. Man in the North-
          east 32:1–34.
Kirch, Patrick V.
  1984    The Evolution of the Polynesian Chiefdoms. Cambridge: Cambridge University
          Press.
Klein, Michael
  1996    Chronology and Interaction among Middle Woodland through Contact Era So-
          cieties in Western Virginia and Maryland: An Evaluation of Ceramic Technology
          and Style. In Upland Archaeology in the East: Symposium VI. Michael B. Barber,
          ed. Pp. 154–180. U.S. Department of Agriculture, Forest Service, Southern Region.
Klein, Michael, and Douglas Sanford
  2004    Analytical Scale and Archaeological Perspectives on the Contact Era in the North-
          ern Neck of Virginia. In Indian and European Contact in Context: The Mid-
          Atlantic Region. Dennis B. Blanton and Julia A. King, eds. Gainesville: University
          Press of Florida.
Kopytoff, Igor
  1986    The Cultural Biography of Things. In The Social Life of Things: Commodities in
          Cultural Perspective. Arjun Appadurai, ed. Pp. 64–93. Cambridge: Cambridge
          University Press.
Kupperman, Karen Ordahl
  1980    Settling with the Indians: The Meeting of English and Indian Cultures in America,
          1580–1640. Totowa, NJ: Rowman and Littlefield.
  1984    Roanoke: The Abandoned Colony. Totowa, NJ: Rowman and Allanheld.
  1995    The Beehive as a Model for Colonial Design. In America in European Conscious-
          ness 1493–1750. Karen Ordahl Kupperman, ed. Pp. 272–294. Chapel Hill: Univer-
          sity of North Carolina Press.
  2000    Indians and English: Facing Off in Early America. Ithaca, NY: Cornell University
          Press.
Lapham, Heather A.
  1995    The Analysis of European Glass Trade Beads Recovered from Monongahela Sites
          in Greene County, Pennsylvania. Report submitted to The Bead Society of
          Greater Washington, Washington, DC.
  2001    More Than "A Few Blew Beads": The Glass and Stone Beads from *Jamestown Re-
          discovery's* 1994–1997 Excavations. Journal of the Jamestown Rediscovery Center 1.
Lemay, J. A. Leo
  1992    Did Pocahontas Save Captain John Smith? Athens: University of Georgia Press.
Lévi-Strauss, Claude
  1969    The Elementary Structures of Kinship. Boston: Beacon Press.
Lewis, Clifford Merle, and Albert J. Loomie
  1953    Spanish Jesuit Mission in Virginia, 1570–1572. Chapel Hill: Published for the Vir-
          ginia Historical Society by the University of North Carolina Press.

Lightfoot, Kent G.

1984 The Occupation Duration of Duncan. *In* The Duncan Site: A Study of the Occupation, Duration, and Settlement Pattern of an Early Mogollon Pithouse Village. Kent Lightfoot, ed. Pp. 47–82. Phoenix: Arizona State University Press.

2005 Indians, Missionaries, and Merchants: The Legacy of Colonial Encounters on the California Frontiers. Berkeley: University of California Press.

Lightfoot, Kent G., and Roberta Jewett

1986 The Shift to Sedentary Life: A Consideration of the Occupation Duration of Early Mogollon Pithouse Villages. *In* Mogollon Variability. Charlotte Benson and Steadman Upham, eds. Pp. 9–44. University Museum, Occasional Papers 15. New Mexico State University, Las Cruces.

Lipsitz, George

1995 A Life in the Struggle: Ivory Perry and the Culture of Opposition. Philadelphia: Temple University Press.

1998 The Possessive Investment in Whiteness: How White People Profit from Identity Politics. Philadelphia: Temple University Press.

Longridge, W. H.

1955 The Spiritual Exercises of Saint Ignatius of Loyola. London: A. R. Mowbray.

Lowery, Woodbury

1911 The Spanish Settlements within the Present Limits of the United States. New York: G. P. Putnam's Sons.

Lyon, Eugene

1976 The Enterprise of Florida: Pedro Menéndez de Avilés and the Spanish Conquest of 1565–1568. Gainesville: University Press of Florida.

1990 The Enterprise of Florida. *In* Columbian Consequences, vol. 2: Archaeological and Historical Perspectives on the Spanish Borderlands East. D. H. Thomas, ed. Pp. 281–296. Washington, DC: Smithsonian Institution.

Malinowski, Bronislaw

1922 Argonauts of the Western Pacific. New York: E. P. Dutton.

Mallios, Seth

1998 In the Hands of "Indian Givers"; Exchange and Violence at Ajacan, Roanoke, and Jamestown. Ph.D. dissertation, Department of Anthropology, University of Virginia, Charlottesville.

2000 At the Edge of the Precipice: Frontier Ventures, Jamestown's Hinterland, and the Archaeology of 44JC802. Richmond: Association for the Preservation of Virginia Antiquities.

2001 Every Artifact Counts. *In* Jamestown Rediscovery VII. William Kelso, ed. Pp. 23–34. Jamestown: Association for the Preservation of Virginia Antiquities.

2004a Exchange and Violence at Ajacan, Roanoke, and Jamestown. *In* Indian and European Contact in Context: The Mid-Atlantic Region. Dennis B. Blanton and Julia A. King, eds. Pp. 126–148. Gainesville: University Press of Florida.

2004b Gift Exchange and the Ossomocomuck Balance of Power: Explaining Carolina

Algonquian Socioeconomic Aberrations at Contact. *In* Searching for the Roanoke Colonies: An Interdisciplinary Collection. E. Thomas Shields and Charles Ewen, eds. North Carolina Department of Cultural Resources, Division of Archives and History, Historical Publications Section.

2005a    Homo Regalos: A Call for Applied Gift Exchange in a Time of Global Commodification, Symbolic Violence, and Bloodshed. International Journal of the Humanities, 2003 1:1485–1490.

2005b    The Creation of Ajacan's Martyrs. *In* The Colonial Chesapeake: New Perspectives. Debra Meyers and Melanie Perreault, eds. Lanham, MD: Lexington Books.

2007    The Apotheosis of Ajacan's Jesuit Missionaries. Ethnohistory (Accepted April 2005).

Mallios, Seth, and Garrett Fesler

1999    Archaeological Excavations at 44JC568, the Reverend Richard Buck Site. Jamestown: Association for the Preservation of Virginia Antiquities.

Mallios, Seth, and Beverly Straube

2000    1999 Interim Report on the APVA Excavations at Jamestown, Virginia. Jamestown: Association for the Preservation of Virginia Antiquities.

Martin, Malachi

1987    The Jesuits: The Society of Jesus and the Betrayal of the Roman Catholic Church. New York: Linden Press, Simon and Schuster.

Marx, Karl, and Friedrich Engels

1977    Capital: A Critique of Political Economy. New York: Vintage Books.

Mauss, Marcel

1990    The Gift. W. D. Halls, trans. New York: W. W. Norton.

1997    Gift, Gift. *In* The Logic of the Gift: Toward an Ethic of Generosity. Alan Schrift, ed. Pp. 28–32. New York: Routledge.

McEwan, B. G.

1993    Spanish Missions of La Florida. Gainesville: University Press of Florida.

1995    Spanish Precedents and Domestic Life at Puerto Real: The Archaeology of Two Spanish Homesites. *In* Puerto Real: The Archaeology of a Sixteenth-Century Spanish Town in Hispaniola. K. Deagan, ed. Pp. 197–230. Gainesville: University Press of Florida.

Merrell, James H.

1979    Cultural Continuity among the Piscataway Indians of Colonial Maryland. William and Mary Quarterly, 3rd series, 36:548–570.

1989    The Indians' New World: Catawbas and Their Neighbors from European Contact through the Era of Removal. Chapel Hill: University of North Carolina Press.

Milanich, Jerald T.

1990    The European Entrada into La Florida: An Overview. *In* Columbian Consequences, vol. 2: Archaeological and Historical Perspectives on the Spanish Borderlands East. D. H. Thomas, ed. Pp. 3–30. Washington, DC: Smithsonian Institution.

1995    Florida Indians and the Invasion from Europe. Gainesville: University Press of Florida.

1999 Laboring in the Fields of the Lord: Spanish Missions and Southeastern Indians. Washington, DC: Smithsonian Institution Press.

Miller, Christopher L., and George R. Hamell

1986 A New Perspective on Indian-White Contact: Cultural Symbols and Colonial Trade. Journal of American History 73(2):311-328.

Miller, Henry M., Dennis J. Pogue, and Michael A. Smolek

1983 Beads from the Seventeenth-Century Chesapeake. Proceedings of the 1982 Glass Bead Conference. Charles F. Hayes, ed. Pp. 127-144, Research Records 16, Rochester Museum and Science Division, Rochester, New York.

Milliken, R.

1995 A Time of Little Choice: The Disintegration of Tribal Culture in the San Francisco Bay Area 1769-1810. Menlo Park, CA: Ballena Press.

Mintz, Sidney

1985 Sweetness and Power: The Place of Sugar in Modern History. New York: Penguin.

Mitchell, Lynette G.

1997 Greeks Bearing Gifts: The Public Use of Private Relationships in the Greek World, 435-323 B.C. Cambridge: Cambridge University Press.

Mitchem, Jeffrey M., and Jonathan M. Leader

1988 Early Sixteenth-Century Beads from Tatham Mound, Citrus County, Florida: Data and Interpretations. Florida Anthropologist 41(1):42-60.

Monahan, Elizabeth I.

1995 Bioarchaeological Analysis of the Mortuary Practices at the Broad Reach Site (31CR218), Coastal North Carolina. North Carolina Archaeology 44:37-69.

Morgan, Edmund S.

1976 American Slavery, American Freedom. New York: Norton.

Monroy, D.

1989 Thrown among Strangers: The Makings of Mexican Culture in Frontier California. Berkeley: University of California Press.

Nemoianu, Virgil

1985 The Selling of Gifts: Another Look at Alienation. Telos 65:311-327.

Noël Hume, Ivor

1994 The Virginia Adventure: Roanoke to James Towne: An Archaeological and Historical Odyssey. New York: A. A. Knopf.

Oberg, Michael Leroy

1999 Dominion and Civility. Ithaca, NY: Cornell University Press.

Obeyesekere, Gananath

1992 The Apotheosis of James Cook: European Mythmaking in the Pacific. Princeton, NJ: Princeton University Press.

Ollman, Bertell

1971 Alienation: Marx's Conception of Man in Capitalist Society. Cambridge: Cambridge University Press.

Otnes, Cele, and Richard F. Beltramini

1996 Gift Giving and Gift Giving: An Overview. In Gift Giving: A Research Anthology.

Cele Otnes and Richard F. Beltramini, eds. Pp. 3–15. Bowling Green, OH: Bowling Green State University Popular Press.

Parry, Jonathan

1986    The Gift, the Indian Gift and the "Indian Gift." Man 21:453–473.

1989    On the Moral Perils of Exchange. In Money and the Morality of Exchange. J. Parry and M. Bloch, eds. Pp. 64–93. Cambridge: Cambridge University Press.

Pearson, Charles

1977    Evidence of Early Spanish Contact on the Georgia Coast. Historical Archaeology 11:74–83.

Percy, George

1967    Observations Gathered out of "A Discourse on the Plantation of the Southern Colony in Virginia by the English, 1606." Charlottesville: Published for the Association for the Preservation of Virginia Antiquities by the University of Virginia Press.

Perdue, Theda

1985    Native Carolinians: The Indians of North Carolina. Raleigh: Division of Archives and History, North Carolina Department of Cultural Resources.

Phillips, G. H.

1975    Chiefs and Challengers: Indian Resistance and Cooperation in Southern California. Berkeley: University of California Press.

Polzer, Charles W.

1976    Rules and Precepts of the Jesuit Missions of Northwestern New Spain. Tucson: University of Arizona Press.

Potter, Stephen

1982    An Analysis of Chicacoan Settlement Patterns. Ph.D. dissertation, Department of Anthropology, University of North Carolina, Chapel Hill.

1989    Early English Effects on Virginia Algonquian Exchange and Tribute in the Tidewater Potomac. In Powhatan's Mantle: Indians in the Colonial Southeast. Peter Wood, Gregory Waselkov, and Thomas Hatley, eds. Pp. 151–172. Lincoln: University of Nebraska Press.

1993    Commoners, Tribute, and Chiefs: The Development of Algonquian Culture in the Potomac Valley. Charlottesville: University of Virginia Press.

Potter, Stephen R., and Gregory Waselkov

1994    Whereby We Shall Enjoy Their Cultivated Places. In Historical Archaeology of the Chesapeake. Barbara J. Little and Paul A. Shackel, eds. Pp. 23–33. Washington, DC: Smithsonian Institution Press.

Price, David A.

2003    Love and Hate in Jamestown: John Smith, Pocahontas, and the Heart of a New Nation. New York: Knopf.

Quinn, David B.

1949    Raleigh and the British Empire. New York: Macmillan.

1970    Thomas Harriot and the Virginia Voyages of 1602. William and Mary Quarterly, 3rd ser., 27:268–281.

1973   Virginia Voyages From Hakluyt. London: Oxford University Press.

1974   England and the Discovery of America, 1481–1620. New York: Knopf.

1977   North America from Earliest Discovery to First Settlements, the Norse Voyages to 1612. New York: Harper and Row/Harper Colophon Books.

1978   The Extension of Settlement in Florida, Virginia, and the Spanish Southwest. New York: Arno Press.

1979a   America from Concept to Discovery. New York: Arno Press.

1979b   English Plans for North America. New York: Arno Press.

1983   England's Sea Empire. London: G. Allen and Unwin.

1984   The Lost Colonists and Their Probable Fate. Raleigh: North Carolina Department of Cultural Resources.

1985   Set Fair for Roanoke, Voyages and Colonies, 1584–1606. Chapel Hill: University of North Carolina Press.

1990   Explorers and Colonies: America, 1500–1625. London: Hambledon Press.

Quinn, David B., ed.

1955   The Roanoke Voyages 1584–1590. Vols. 1–2. London: Hakluyt Society.

1971   North American Discovery. Columbia: University of South Carolina Press.

1979c   New American World, a Documentary History of North America to 1612. Vols. 1–5. New York: Arno Press and Hector Bye.

1994   The European Outthrust and Encounter: The First Phase c. 1400–c. 1700: Essays in Tribute to David Beers Quinn on his 85th Birthday. Liverpool: Liverpool University Press.

Quinn, David Beers, and A. N. Ryan

1983   England's Sea Empire, 1550–1642. Boston: G. Allen and Unwin.

Quitt, Martin H.

1995   Trade and Acculturation at Jamestown, 1607–1609: The Limits of Understanding. William and Mary Quarterly, 3rd ser., 52(2):227–258.

Redmond, Elisa M.

1998   Introduction: The Dynamics of Chieftaincy and the Development of Chiefdoms. *In* Chiefdoms and Chieftaincy in the Americas. Elisa Redmond, ed. Pp. 1–17. Gainesville: University Press of Florida.

Roberts, Michael

1997   Histories. International Social Science Journal 153:373–385.

Ross, Lester A.

1974   Hudson's Bay Company Glass Trade Beads: Manufacturing Types Imported to Fort Vancouver (1829–1960). Bead Journal 1(2):15–22.

Rountree, Helen

1989   The Powhatan Indians of Virginia: Their Traditional Culture. Norman: University of Oklahoma Press.

1990   Pocahontas's People: The Powhatan Indians of Virginia Through Four Centuries. Norman: University of Oklahoma Press.

Rountree, Helen, ed.

1993   Powhatan Foreign Relations, 1500–1722. Charlottesville: University of Virginia Press.

Rountree, Helen, and Thomas Davidson

1997     Eastern Shore Indians of Virginia and Maryland. Charlottesville: University of Virginia Press.

Rountree, Helen, and E. Randolph Turner III

1998     The Evolution of the Powhatan Paramount Chiefdom in Virginia. *In* Chiefdoms and Chieftaincy in the Americas. Elisa Redmond, ed. Pp. 265–296. Gainesville: University Press of Florida.

2002     Before and After Jamestown: Virginia's Powhatans and Their Predecessors. Gainesville: University Press of Florida.

Sahlins, Marshall David

1972     Stone Age Economics. Chicago: Aldine-Atherton.

1981     Historical Metaphors and Mythical Realities: Structure in the Early History of the Sandwich Island Kingdom. Ann Arbor: University of Michigan Press.

1985     Islands of History. Chicago: University of Chicago Press.

1995     How "Natives" Think: About Captain Cook, For Example. Chicago: University of Chicago Press.

Sandys, George

1613     Description of the Turkish Empire. London: W. Barrett.

Schwerin, Karl H.

1973     The Anthropological Antecedents: Caciques, Cacicazgos, and Caciquismo. *In* The Caciques: Oligarchical Politics and the System of Caciquismo in the Luso-Hispanic World. R. Kern, ed. Pp. 5–17. Albuquerque: University of New Mexico Press.

Service, Elman Rogers

1962     Primitive Social Organization: An Evolutionary Perspective. New York: Random House.

Shapiro, Gary

1997     The Metaphysics of Presents: Nietzsche's Gift, the Debt to Emerson, Heidegger's Values. *In* The Logic of the Gift: Toward an Ethic of Generosity. Alan Schrift, ed. Pp. 274–291. New York: Routledge.

Sheehan, Bernard

1980     Savagism and Civility: Indians and Englishmen in Colonial Virginia. Cambridge: Cambridge University Press.

Smith, John, Philip L. Barbour, and Institute of Early American History and Culture

1986     The Complete Works of Captain John Smith (1580–1631). 3 Vols. Chapel Hill: Published for the Institute of Early American History and Culture, Williamsburg VA, by the University of North Carolina Press.

Smith, Marvin T.

1976     The Chevron Trade Bead in North America. Bead Journal 3(1):15–17.

1983     Chronology from Glass Beads: The Spanish Period in the Southeast, c. A.D. 1513–1670. Proceedings of the 1982 Glass Bead Conference. Charles F. Hayes, ed. Pp. 147–158. Research Records 16, Rochester Museum and Science Division, Rochester, NY.

Smith, Marvin T., and Mary Elizabeth Good
   1982    Early Seventeenth-Century Glass Beads in the Spanish Colonial Trade. Cotton-
           landia Museum Publications, Greenwood, MS.
Spelman, Henry
   1872    Relation of Virginia. London: Chiswick Press.
Spicer, Edward Holland
   1962    Cycles of Conquest: The Impact of Spain, Mexico, and the United States on the
           Indians of the Southwest, 1533–1960. Tucson: University of Arizona Press.
Stirrat, R. L.
   1989    Money, Men and Women. *In* Money and the Morality of Exchange. J. Parry and
           M. Bloch, eds. Pp. 94–116. Cambridge: Cambridge University Press.
Strachey, William
   1953    The Historie of Travell into Virginia Britania (1612). London: Printed for the
           Hakluyt Society.
Strathern, Marilyn
   1988    The Gender of the Gift. Berkeley: University of California Press.
   1992    Qualified Value: The Perspective of Gift Exchange. *In* Barter, Exchange and Value:
           An Anthropological Approach. Caroline Humphrey and Stephen Hughes-Jones,
           eds. Pp. 169–191. Cambridge: Cambridge University Press.
Taylor, Alan
   2001    American Colonies. New York: Viking.
Thomas, David Hurst
   1988    Saints and Soldiers at Santa Catalina: Hispanic Designs for Colonial America. *In*
           The Recovery of Meaning. Mark P. Leone and Parker B. Potter, eds. Pp. 73–140.
           Washington, DC: Smithsonian Institution Press.
   1990    The Spanish Missions of La Florida: An Overview. *In* Columbian Consequences,
           vol. 2: Archaeological and Historical Perspectives on the Spanish Borderlands
           East. D. H. Thomas, ed. Pp. 357–398. Washington, DC: Smithsonian Institution.
Thomas, Nicholas
   1991    Entangled Objects: Exchange, Material Culture, and Colonialism in the Pacific.
           Cambridge, MA: Harvard University Press.
Todorov, Tzvetan
   1984    The Conquest of America: The Question of the Other. New York: Harper and
           Row.
Townsend, Camilla
   2004    Pocahontas and the Powhatan Dilemma. New York: Hill and Wang.
Turner, E. Randolph, III
   1976    An Archaeological and Ethnohistorical Study on the Evolution of Rank Societies
           in the Virginia Coastal Plain. Ph.D. dissertation, Department of Anthropology,
           Pennsylvania State University, University Park.
   1978    Population Distribution in the Virginia Coastal Plain, 8000 B.C. to A.D. 1600. Ar-
           chaeology of Eastern North America 6:60–72.

1982    A Re-Examination of Powhatan Territorial Boundaries and Population, ca. A.D. 1607. Quarterly Bulletin of the Archaeological Society of Virginia.

1985    Socio-Political Organization within the Powhatan Chiefdom and the Effects of European Contact, A.D. 1607–1646. *In* Cultures in Contact: The Impact of European Contacts on Native American Cultural Institutions, A.D. 1000–1800. William W. Fitzhugh, ed. Pp. 193–224. Washington, DC: Smithsonian Institution Press.

1986    Difficulties in the Archaeological Identification of Chiefdoms as Seen in the Virginia Coastal Plain during the Late Woodland and Early Historic Periods. *In* Late Woodland Cultures of the Middle Atlantic Region. Jay F. Custer, ed. Pp. 19–28. Newark: University of Delaware Press.

1993    Native American Protohistoric Interactions in the Powhatan Core Area. *In* Powhatan Foreign Relations, 1500–1722. Helen Rountree, ed. Pp. 76–93. Charlottesville: University of Virginia Press.

VanDerWarker, Amber M.

2001    An Archaeological Study of Late Woodland Fauna in the Roanoke River Basin. North Carolina Archaeology 50:1–46.

Wagner, M. J.

1998    Some Think It Impossible to Civilize Them at All: Cultural Change and Continuity among the Early Nineteenth-Century Potawatomi. *In* Studies in Culture Contact: Interaction, Culture Change, and Archaeology. J. G. Cusick, ed. Pp. 430–456. Occasional Paper No. 25. Carbondale: Center for Archaeological Investigations, Southern Illinois University.

Wallerstein, I.

1974    The Modern World System I. New York: Academic Press.

1980    The Modern World System II. New York: Academic Press.

1989    The Modern World System III. New York: Academic Press.

Ward, H. Trawick, and R. P. Stephen Davis

1999    Time before History: The Archaeology of North Carolina. Chapel Hill: University of North Carolina Press.

Waselkov, Gregory A.

1989    Introduction: Politics and Economics. *In* Powhatan's Mantle: Indians in the Colonial Southeast. Peter H. Wood, Gregory A. Waselkov, and M. Thomas Hatley, eds. Pp. 129–133. Lincoln: University of Nebraska Press.

Webb, Stephen Saunders

1979    The Governors-General: The English Army and the Definition of the Empire, 1569–1681. Chapel Hill: Published for the Institute of Early American History and Culture by the University of North Carolina Press.

Weber, David

1992    The Spanish Frontier in North America. New Haven, CT: Yale University Press.

Weiner, Annette B.

1992    Inalienable Possessions: The Paradox of Keeping-While-Giving. Berkeley: University of California Press.

White, Richard
  1991    The Middle Ground: Indians, Empires, and Republics in the Great Lakes Region, 1650–1815. Cambridge: Cambridge University Press.

Williamson, Margaret Holmes
  1979    Powhatan Hair. Man 14:392–413.
  1992    Pocahontas and Captain John Smith: Examining a Historical Myth. History and Anthropology 5(3–4):365–402.
  2003    Powhatan Lords of Life and Death: Command and Consent in Seventeenth-Century Virginia. Lincoln: University of Nebraska Press.

Wolf, Eric R.
  1997    Europe and the People without History. 2nd ed. Berkeley: University of California Press.

Wray, Charles F.
  1983    Seneca Glass Trade Beads c. A.D. 1550–1820. Proceedings of the 1982 Glass Bead Conference. Charles F. Hayes, ed. Pp. 41–49, Research Records 16, Rochester Museum and Science Division, Rochester, NY.

Wright, Henry
  1984    Prestate Political Formations. *In* On the Evolution of Complex Societies: Essays in Honor of Harry Hoijer 1982. Timothy Earle, ed. Pp. 41–78. Malibu, CA: Undena.

# Index

abandonment by Algonquians: of colonists at Jamestown, 82–86, 90–92, 94–98; of colonists at Roanoke, 69–71; of missionaries at Ajacan, 2, 22, 38, 47–52, 55, 118

Abbot, John S. C., 115

Age of Exploration, 1, 16

Ajacan, 1–9, 17, 21–23, 31, 58–59, 69, 80–81, 83, 107, 113, 114, 115, 118, 119, 120–121, 122; amicability with missionaries, 44–49; attack on missionaries, 37, 52–53; history and pre-trade activity, 36–44; food procurement from, 114; as second Eden, 114; Spanish retribution towards, 53–57; trade and morality, 114–116

Albemarle Sound, 15, 66, 67

Alexander VI, Pope, 38

Algonquian culture, 9, 17; culture clash with Europeans, 21–24; prestige exchange and European goods, 17–21; and public embarrassment, 22, 51–52, 83, 104, 120; rationale for trade with Spanish, 39; hierarchy disrupted due to trade, 112; symbolic violence, 3, 102, 120–122; tribute system, 17

Algonquian Indians: 9, 15, 118; attack on Spanish under Don Luis 1–3; of the Carolinas, 15–17; desire for metal and metal goods, 18–21; general exchange pattern with Europeans, 117–123; gift exchange, 4–5. *See also* Arrohattoc Indians; Chawanoac Indians; Chesepian Indians; Chickahominy Indi-

ans; Croatoan Indians; Kecoughtan Indians; Kiskiak Indians; Mattaponi Indians; Moratuc Indians; Ossomocomuck Indians; Pamunkey Indians; Paspahegh Indians; Powhatan Indians; Quiyoughcohannock Indians; Sectoan Indians; Weanock Indians; Weapemeoc Indians; Youghtanund Indians

Alligator River, 15

Altamirano, Hernando de, 7, 61

Amadas, Philip, 59–62

antimony ore, 17

Appamattuck Indians, 83

Appocant, 86, 104

Aquascococke (village), 73, 79, 82; silver cup incident, 63–65

Archer, Gabriel, 8, 9, 110

Arrohattoc (village), 83

Arrohattoc Indians, 83, 104

Baptista (Mendez), Brother Juan, 43, 50

Barlowe, Arthur, 7, 18, 59–62, 109, 116

Binford, Lewis, 13

Blanton, Dennis, 23

bread, 61, 85, 93, 120

Buck, Richard, 103

Busbecq, Ogier Ghislain de, 8

Capahowasick, 88, 90, 104

Cape Henry, 81

# Suggested Reading

A. Bowdoin Van Riper, *Edgartown*, Arcadia Pub., 2018

Allen, Joseph C., *Tails and Trails of Martha's Vineyard*, Little, Brown and Co., 1938

Banks, Charles E. & Dean, George H., *The History of Martha's Vineyard Dukes County Vol II Town Annals*, George H. Dean, 1911

Dresser, Thos., *Hidden History of Martha's Vineyard*, The History Press, 2017

Foster, David R., *A Meeting of Land and Sea*, Yale University Press, 2017

Gookin, Warner Foote, B.D, *Capawack alias Martha's Vineyard*, Dukes County Historical Society, Edgartown MA, 1947

Hine, C. G., *The Story of Martha's Vineyard*, Hine Bros., 1908

Hough, Henry Beetle, *Martha's Vineyard; Summer Resort 1835-1935*, Tuttle Pub., 1936

Hough, Henry Beetle, *Singing in the Morning and Other Essays About Martha's Vineyard*, Simon and Schuster, 1951

Huntington, Gale, *An Introduction to Martha's Vineyard*, Martha's Vineyard Print Co., 1969

Martha's Vineyard Commission, *Island Plan; Charting the Future of the Vineyard*, MV Commission, 2010

No author given, *Fifty Glimpses of Martha's Vineyard*, Rand McNally, 1900

Simon, Anne W., *No Island Is an Island, The Ordeal of Martha's Vineyard*, Doubleday and Company, 1973

Railton, Arthur R., *The History of Martha's Vineyard*, Commonwealth Editions, 2006

Safford, Nancy, *Time's Island, Portraits of the Vineyard*, MIT Press, 1973

Simon, Peter, *On the Vineyard*, Anchor Books, 1980

Smith, Wayne and Stacy, Bonnie, *Island Stories*, Martha's Vineyard Museum, 2015

Weiss, Ellen, *City in the Woods*, Oxford University Press, 1987

# ACKNOWLEDGEMENTS

First, I thank Bow Van Riper of the Martha's Vineyard Museum for his hospitality and the unflagging support that has made this book possible. Christine Seidel of the Martha's Vineyard Commission provided the necessary cartographic tools, and Hilary Wall of the *Vineyard Gazette* the background story to much of what is contained within. Durwood Vanderhoop also kindly assisted with Wampanoag translation.

In traveling around the island to secure the contemporary photographs, I was frequently assisted by island residents themselves. I thank Donna Leon, Robert Gatchell, Doug Thomson, Tim Donahue, Aesha Mumin, Sarah Keena, Bill Roman, Thomas Fisher, Kathryn Allen, Dick Miller, Kevin L. Searle, John and Diane Maguire, Harold Chapdelaine, Robin Wilson, Nancy Crossley Black and Mark Wallace. Their warm receptions and eagerness to help made this project much less taxing and much more memorable.

# PHOTO AND MAP CREDITS

| | |
|---|---|
| hne | Historic New England |
| loc | Library of Congress |
| macris | Courtesy Office of the Secretary of the Commonwealth William F. Galvin, Massachusetts Historical Commission |
| mvc | Maps compiled by Chris Seidel of the Martha's Vineyard Commission, 2019 |
| mvm | Martha's Vineyard Museum |

**FRONT COVER**
Top: mvm
Bottom: the author

**BACK COVER**
Top: detail from image page 17
Bottom: the author